INCLUDING A WILDFLOWER IDENTIFICATION CHAPTER

Hiking Trail

◇12 ⬌	PIKA'S TRAVERSE
◉ →	TO GONDOLA 0.9km
🍴 ←	TO HARMONY TEA HOUSE 1.3km
◉ ←	TO PEAK CHAIR 2.3km
5 ↗	T-BAR TRAIL 0.6km

PACK IT OUT.
PACK IT BACK.

QUICKDRAW
PUBLICATIONS

BY BRIAN FINESTONE & KEVIN HODDER

DISCLAIMER:

READ THIS BEFORE YOU USE THIS BOOK!

Hiking is a sport with inherent risks. Participating in this sport may result in injury or death.

This guidebook is intended for hikers with a degree of ability and experience. The terrain described within can be dangerous and requires a high level of fitness and attention to negotiate. This guidebook is a compilation of information from several sources. As a result the authors cannot confirm the accuracy of any specific detail. Difficulty ratings are subjective and may vary depending on your own personal experience and the conditions on the trail. There may be misinformation in regards to hike descriptions, conditions, difficulties or any other detail. This guidebook does not give the user the right to access any terrain described within. The Municipality and any other land owner or land manager may limit access to any part of a trail at any time. It is your responsibility to adhere to all closures.

PUBLISHER
Quickdraw Publications
Post Office Box 5313
Squamish, British Columbia
Canada V8B 0C2

CONTACT US
(604) 892-9271
info@quickdrawpublications.com
www.quickdrawpublications.com

Quickdraw Publications is constantly expanding our range of guidebooks. If you have a manuscript or an idea for a book, or would like to find out more about our company, please get in touch.

Books printed in China.

WHISTLER HIKING GUIDE - FIRST EDITION

INTERNATIONAL STANDARD BOOK NUMBER
978-0-9732593-5-3

AUTHORS
Brian Finestone and Kevin Hodder.

BOOK PHOTOGRAPHY
All photographs by the authors unless otherwise noted.

COVER PHOTOGRAPHY
Front cover photograph of summer hiking on Blackcomb mountain by Brian Finestone. Back cover photograph of hiker leaping at sunset by Brian Finestone. Back cover photograph of Red Columbine flower by Kevin Hodder.

QUICKDRAW PUBLICATIONS

GUIDEBOOKS FOR OUTDOOR ADVENTURES

ROCK CLIMBING   HIKING   MOUNTAIN BIKING   SKIING

CONTENTS

Scenic wonder *Taking in the view from the first summit of the Stawamus Chief.*

Welcome to Whistler *Enjoying the evening alpine sun while hiking on Blackcomb Mountain.*

INTRODUCTION

Whistler is an idyllic mountain community nestled in the heart of British Columbia's Coast Mountains. The townsite rests in a broad, forested valley punctuated by aquamarine lakes and dramatic, snowcapped peaks. Whistler's scenic beauty is breathtaking and, for mountain recreation, it's one of North America's premier destinations.

Skiers despair as winter loosens it's frosty grip on Whistler valley, but the warmth of spring unveils a world-class selection of mountain trails. From broad, cobbled walkways meandering through the village to backcountry treks in lush alpine meadows, Whistler has it all. This valley is a haven for hiking enthusiasts and this guidebook outlines the premier outdoor walking experiences in this part of beautiful, British Columbia. Enjoy, and tread lightly!

GETTING TO WHISTLER

The Resort Municipality of Whistler is nestled in a valley alongside Highway 99, approximately 120 km north of the metropolitan city of Vancouver. Highway 99 begins at the United States border and meanders through Vancouver before striking northward into the heart of British Columbia. The portion of Highway 99 that accesses Whistler is reached via Highway 1, which runs adjacent to the seaside community of Horseshoe Bay. First-time visitors to Whistler are encouraged to obtain a map of BC and Vancouver to help navigate.

Marina reflection *Late-day light illuminates the waterfront adjacent to downtown Vancouver. This vibrant city is framed by mountains to the north and the Pacific Ocean to the west.*

Sea-to-Sky *Highway 99 is the gateway to Whistler. Breathtaking views distract first-time travellers along the road. The highway rolls through the historic mining community of Britannia Beach and the "Outdoor Recreation Capital of Canada", Squamish.*

AROUND TOWN

Whistler has a permanent population of approximately 10,000, plus a larger population of seasonal workers. Over two million people visit Whistler annually, primarily for alpine skiing and mountain biking. The village has won numerous design awards and Whistler has been voted among the top destinations in North America by major ski magazines since the mid-1990s. Hotels and restaurants abound and visitors are encouraged to contact the local chamber of commerce to help with options.

Valley living *Whistler Village is nestled in a valley between two world-famous ski areas, Blackcomb and Whistler. This photo crops out the majority of Whistler Mountain on the right, but the upper bowls of Blackcomb are clearly visible on the left.*

European Inspiration *Local architecture is often modeled after the quaint stone villages found in the French and Swiss Alps.*

HIKING SAFETY

Although hiking is considered to be one of the lower risk outdoor activities in the area, there is some potential for mishaps. A few basic principles can help you manage the objective hazards.

1 PRE-HIKE PREPARATION

Many factors, such as weather and trail condition need to be considered when choosing a hike. The Whistler Blackcomb website (Whistlerblackcomb.com) links to the Environment Canada weather forecast for both the Whistler valley and alpine areas. These links will give you the forecast high and low temperatures and the probability of precipitation, which are very helpful in selecting adequate clothing for your outing.

Sometimes you have to be a bit of a detective to find information on the condition of trails. In the early season, for instance, the big question is whether a trail is free of snow or not. For hikes within Garibaldi Provincial Park, there is an excellent trail update available on the BC Parks website on the Garibaldi Park page. If you are planning on hiking on Whistler or Blackcomb, information can be gained by consulting Guest Relations at the bottom of the lift. It may also be helpful to inquire at a local outdoor store such as Escape Route in the Marketplace. The staff is usually pretty knowledgeable and helpful.

Research *Preparation pays off.*

Generally, low-level trails in the Whistler valley can be free of snow by early April. By late May, the snow level is usually above the 1,100 meter mark thus opening up a wide variety of sub-alpine trails. By mid July, the alpine hikes are usually melting quickly and opening up. The other end of the season can be much less predictable. Snow can arrive in the valley in late October or stay away until December.

Regardless, if you find that the trail you were hoping to hike that day is covered with snow, it's probably a good idea to leave it for another day. Staying on a trail can be extremely difficult if it is covered with snow. As well, remaining snow may make for very difficult footing and in specific terrain features, indicate that an avalanche hazard could exist.

Prior to venturing off, make sure someone responsible knows your itinerary. Prepare a route card with the details of your intended hike and any alternatives you might take. Include your estimated time of departure and return, a list of what you brought with you and the details of the other people along for the hike. Ensure that you leave your route card with someone who will realize that you are overdue from your trip and will notify the authorities.

2 EQUIPMENT

Surprise *Zhiggy's Meadow in summer.*

☐ **Clothing:** You can literally experience the weather of all four seasons on any given day in Whistler. This can make choosing clothing a difficult task. Savvy hikers plan on everyday having the possibility of rain and bring a waterproof jacket just in case. Also, remember not to be comforted by the temperatures in the valley when you plan to hike in the alpine. Some of the hikes in this book will take you 1,500 meters above Whistler Village! Consider that air moving up a mountain cools at a rate of 6 degrees Celsius per 1,000 meters. What this equates to is the mountaintops being about 10 degrees Celsius cooler than the village! Therefore, bring extra warm clothes and a warm hat. Remember, you can always take them off if you get hot!

Follow the general guidelines of dressing in layers and avoiding cotton garments. Simply explained, when cotton gets wet, it stays wet next to the skin. Wet clothes next to the skin mean a cold body. A cold body can lead to a rapid onset of hypothermia!

☐ **Water:** Safe sources of drinking water do exist in the backcountry however, so do sources infested with the parasite *Giardia*. The only way to be sure of avoiding contaminated water is to fill your container from a known source or purify the water. Packs with built-in hydration systems are virtually the norm now and make carrying a few liters of water fairly painless. If you choose to purify, there are many portable water treatment systems available.

☐ **Food:** You're going to be burning calories out there so bring plenty of portable snacks and allow for the hike to take longer than you may expect. Trail mix, energy bars, nuts and dried fruit are popular hiking fare and are available all over town.

☐ **Sunscreen, Hat and Sunglasses:** Remember, ultraviolet radiation is more severe in the alpine than at sea level. And you wouldn't go to the beach without these things now would you?

☐ **Cell Phones:** Cell phones can be a vital tool in case of an emergency however there are vast areas where cell phones cannot obtain a signal in and around the Whistler area. In areas where service is intermittent or non-existent, a cell phone will automatically switch to a mode that continually scans for service. This mode uses considerably more battery power and can waste valuable airtime in the event of an emergency. The best way to pack a cell phone for emergency purposes is turned-off and sealed in a zip-lock bag. Emergency numbers include:

- Ambulance, Police, Fire: 911
- Whistler Medical Clinic: (604) 932-4911
- Whistler Blackcomb Patrol: (604) 938-7720

☐ **Map / Compass / Altimeter / GPS:** Yes, the trails described within this guidebook are all established routes that generally require little in the way of navigation. That being said, it can enrich your trip to have the topographic map for the area and be able to identify the peaks, lakes and rivers that you see along the way. It also never hurts to know exactly where you are on the map at all times in case of an emergency. We provide GPS waypoints for the trailheads for each hike and having a handheld GPS can assist in finding the start of your hike.

☐ **Head Light or Flash Light:** Carrying a light source has become increasingly easy with the popularity of LED technology. Small lights weigh mere grams and can be stashed away in your pack where they remain unnoticed until they're needed. Having walked off the summit of the Stawamus Chief in the pitch black with only the dim glow of a wristwatch to light the way, we can attest to the value of a proper light source!

☐ **First Aid Kit:** Ask someone to show you a backcountry first aid kit and you can see anything from a massive expedition pack to a small zip-lock baggie with a few band-aids and some duct tape. What do you really need? For most short hiking trips all that is necessary is something to help relieve blisters and small lacerations.

Joffre Lakes *Remote hikes require careful preparations*

Include a space blanket, matches, some medical tape and two triangular bandages and you'll be able to handle *most* situations encountered on a hike.

☐ **Duct Tape:** Ah, the "silver saviour", second only to water as being the most useful substance on earth! Obvious uses include the repair of clothing, glasses, backpacks, water carriers, boots, etc. Duct tape can also be used in the construction of an emergency shelter, splints and even crutches. Perhaps one of the favored uses among mountaineers is blister prevention. By applying a patch of duct tape to the heel area and smoothing out any wrinkles, one can extend the life of skin on high friction points and delay the onset of blisters.

3 HAZARDS

☐ **Mountain Bikes:** Some of the trails in this book were originally built by (and for) mountain bikers. Officially, the right-of-way should be given to hikers, however for your safety we recommend stepping off the trail as soon as you hear or see an approaching bike. Trails used by mountain bikers are designated in this guide as a warning of potential high-speed traffic. These trails may also have bridges and boardwalks that were designed for bikes and must carefully be used by hikers.

☐ **Bears:** Whistler is home to a flourishing population of black bears *(Ursus americanus)* along with many inventive programs to allow for human-wildlife coexistence. We encourage everyone to consult Bearsmart.com. It is an excellent source of information on bears and bear safety. Becoming familiar with the extensive advice posted on this site before recreating in bear country is extremely worthwhile. It is important to realize that every bear encounter is unique and there are no steadfast rules that can be applied in every situation. Here are some generally accepted practices:

- It is considered safer to hike in groups in bear country.
- When hiking, stay alert. Look for bears and signs of bear activity.
- Avoid surprising a bear. Talk or sing when hiking so that you not only warn the bears of your presence but also identify yourself as human.
- If you see a bear, don't approach it. Remain calm, speak in a calm voice, avoid direct eye contact and back away slowly. *Never* approach a bear!
- If a bear approaches you, don't panic! Talk firmly and wave your hands above your head in an effort to make yourself appear like a larger presence. Continue to leave the area.
- Many people advise carrying bear pepper spray in case of attack. It is important to educate yourself in the safe transport and use of the spray if you choose to carry it.
- Remember that bears have the right-of-way in Whistler whether on a trail, road or fairway!

"Bears are far more likely to enhance your wilderness experience than spoil it! Knowing how to interpret their behavior and act responsibly is part of the thrill of sharing forests and mountains with these amazing creatures."
  – Bearsmart.com

☐ **Bees:** There is a variety of ground dwelling wasps or "yellowjackets" in British Columbia that pose a threat to hikers. These stinging insects nest in cavities in dead wood or in holes in the ground. Some years, when conditions are right, they can become abundant during the main hiking season in late summer and fall. Yellowjackets only sting defensively and won't attack unprovoked. The problem is that hikers who disturb a colony unknowingly will unleash their wrath. Unlike regular wasps that sting and quickly depart, these ground-dwellers can engage their victims with their mandibles and sting repeatedly. The result of a yellowjacket encounter may include being stung several times. Hikers with suspected allergic reactions should carry the appropriate medication.

Moving Water *Approaching Rainbow Lake via a small stream crossing.*

☐ **Alpine Hazards:** While travel in the forest is enjoyable, the ultimate reward for many hikers is the portion of trail above the treeline. It is often in this alpine environment where the views are most spectacular and hikers can get a closer view of glacial ice that was formed millions of years ago. In an environment where snow remains year-round, the climate is often harsh and unforgiving. Snow, ice and wet rock all create serious slip and fall hazards. Tread carefully and remember you're a long way from help!

☐ **Moving Water:** Some of the hikes in this book require you to cross small creeks with the use of stepping-stones. Moving water and slimy rocks can pose a hazard. The streams in this corridor are mostly snowmelt or glacier-fed and are extremely cold year-round. Slipping into a stream can be a frigid and dangerous experience. Don't attempt to cross any stream that you are not certain you are capable of.

☐ **Short Cuts:** Short cuts can be blamed for 90% of lost hiker situations and a good portion of hiking related accidents. The misconception that a bushwhack from point A to point B will be faster can ultimately result in negative situations. Short-cuts also have a destructive impact on the environment, but that's discussed in the next section.

HIKING ETHICS

The ethics of hiking revolve around treating our natural ecosystem with the respect it deserves. If we are all determined to hike in a responsible fashion, we will leave these areas with a minimal impact for future generations to enjoy.

- ☐ **Pack It In, Pack It Out:** It's simple enough. If you bring anything into the backcountry it is your responsibility to carry it back out—orange peels included!

- ☐ **Stay on the Maintained Trails:** Sticking to the trails is an essential habit. Short-cutting switchbacks causes devastating erosion and destroy vegetation. In delicate alpine meadows, straying from the trail means that you are trampling fragile vegetation, and, due to the harsh environment and short growing season, this vegetation can take years to recover from such neglect. Remember, the switchbacks are designed to provide an efficient and elegant pathway on which to gain and lose elevation. Use them!

  If a trail is muddy, resist the temptation to spread out and walk around the mud. If enough people follow your course around the mud, the trail will get wider and wider, thus increasing the impact on the area. Besides, wandering around Whistler Village with muddy boots will give you instant credibility!

- ☐ **Human Waste:** What are the implications and ramifications of defecation in outdoor recreation? Well, simply put, human waste can cause devastating effects on the waterways. Some basic guidelines can reduce our impact.

  - If there is an outhouse, please use it.
  - If there is not an outhouse, the most-accepted method of disposing with human waste in the backcountry is carrying it out or burying it 15 centimeters deep and 100 meters from any water source.
  - As for urination, make sure you are off the trail and 60 meters away from a water source.

McGillivray Pass Lodge

Alpine hiking in the heart of the Chilcotin Mountains

Alpine Hiking at its Finest

Join us at our spectacular backcountry lodge deep in the heart of the Chilcotin Wilderness. Experience the magic of this mountain valley, surrounded by soaring peaks and stunning alpine meadows. We offer fantastic hiking on alpine ridges and through meadows of wildflowers with un-parralled views of peaks and glacial lakes. Come visit us for a night or two and enjoy the unspoiled beauty and wilderness of the Chilcotin backcountry.

McGillivray Pass Lodge is a quick helicopter flight from Pemberton, which is located only 2.5 hours from Vancouver and 25 min from Whistler. We offer guiding services and fully catered meals.

mcgillivraypasslodge.com   TOLL FREE 1 888 863 9757   info@mcgillivraypasslodge.com

HOW TO USE THIS GUIDEBOOK

This guide is the ultimate reference for hikers, walkers and trail runners wishing to get the most out of their Whistler experience. The trails are arranged from south to north and each page contains a wealth of information to help you plan your excursion.

Each individual hike is assigned a **trail number**, which then corresponds to a detailed topographical map of that area. To aid in selection, a **quality rating** is provided (one to three stars) and to track your outings, each trail has a corresponding **tick box**. Underneath the trail name is a list of **hiking statistics**. From left to right, these are: *total* hiking distance (car to car), elevation *change* (lowest point on trail to highest), typical months the trail is snow-free and GPS coordinates for the trailhead. The **Hiking** paragraphs underneath the statistics line provide information regarding the nature of the hike along with key tips for staying on route.

Each trail contains an **elevation graph** that provides information about the distance of the trail versus the change in elevation. To emphasize relief, a vertical exaggeration of 2 has been used (i.e., each meter travelled horizontally equals 2 meters on the verti-

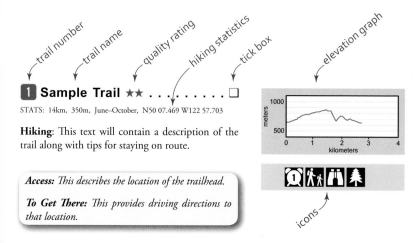

1 **Sample Trail** ★★ . . . . □

STATS: 14km, 350m, June–October, N50 07.469 W122 57.703

Hiking: This text will contain a description of the trail along with tips for staying on route.

Access: This describes the location of the trailhead.

To Get There: This provides driving directions to that location.

HOW TO USE THIS GUIDEBOOK

cal axis). Whether you prefer a short, flat stroll or a steep, marathon of a workout, this should aid in your selection. In addition to the graph, each trail has a corresponding blue **icon** box with a variety of hiking-related symbols. At a glance, these icons provide basic information regarding trail type and features. The clock icon indicates the *estimated* number of hours the hike takes to walk from car to car. Time estimates do not include break times and actual travel times can vary greatly between groups. *Please refer to the icon key on page 20 for specific definitions.*

Each trail page contains a yellow box that holds critical information for finding the trailhead. The *location* of each trailhead is found in the **Access** paragraph; the specific *directions* for finding the trailhead are located in the **To Get There** paragraph.

Driving directions: All driving directions start at the intersection of Highway 99 and Village Gate Boulevard, which is the main entrance to Whistler Village. At this intersection, set your odometer to zero and carefully follow the driving directions to the trailhead. Variations among vehicles may cause slight differences in odometer readings.

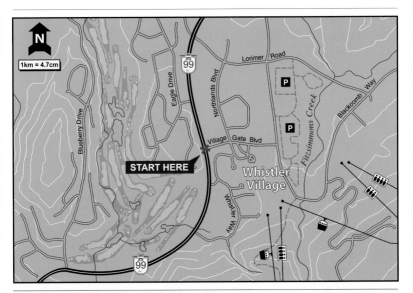

ICON KEY

The card below contains basic descriptions for the icons used in this book. The icons provide a visual reference for the unique characteristics of each hike.

⬆	One way hike	🏞	Waterfall
⬇⬆	Return on same trail	❀	Wildflowers
🔄	Trail follows loop	🔭	Great views
1	Hiking time in hours	👫	Wide track
🚗	Rough road	🛣	Paved trail
🏃	Good trail run	🚫🐕	No dogs
🚲	Watch for bikes	★	Average trail
👫	Good family hike	★★	Very good trail
🌲	Giant trees	★★★	Excellent trail

CONTOUR MAP LEGEND

All the trails in this book are represented on contour maps to provide a general overview of the land along with any prominent features. These contour maps contain white lines (the contours) that show detailed undulations in the terrain. The contours are labelled in meters and, for the experienced user, this can provide information about the steepness and nature of each hike. Each map also contains a directional arrow that points to north and a small scale key to help approximate distances between points on the map.

The adjacent card lists the main features on the maps along with an example of each feature.

Featured Hiking Trail	- - - - -
Other Trails in Area	——
Highway 99	▬▬
Paved Road	▭
Gravel Road	▪ ▪ ▪ ▪
Railway Tracks	▥
Transmission Lines	◇
Contour Line (meters)	— 800 —
Bridge	⌣
Lake	⬤
Creek	
River	
Direction of North	▶N
Scale Key (sample)	1km = 4.7km

We'll take you places no book can.

You're here for a good time, not a long time. Make the most of every moment with guided experiences from the Core. Under the canopy of an old growth forest a challenge awaits, with a **Family Wilderness Tour.** Explore technology as you navigate with one of our **GPS Clinics.** If you want to take your fitness to the next level, join us for a **Trail Running Clinic.** For the ultimate Whistler high, experience our **Outdoor Rock Climbing Tours,** beginner to expert. Our **Climbing Gym and Fitness Centre** is also open daily for drop-in. So call us and write your own epic adventure.

the Core

CLIMBING · FITNESS · STRENGTH

Location: Telus Conference Centre, Whistler - Lower Level, across from Tapley's

METRIC CONVERSION CHART

The following chart is provided for those that are more familiar with imperial units than with metric units.

Key calculations for this book are driving distances to trailheads, overall hiking distances and elevation changes. Use the following formulas to do metric conversions of your own:

- kilometers x 0.62 = miles
- meters x 3.28 = feet

Note: The longest hike with the greatest elevation *change* in this book is Singing Pass Trail, which moves through 1,441 m of changing elevation over 27.8 km. Note that much of this elevation change is downhill as most hikers ride the lift to the trailhead, but hike down to the valley at day's end. The hike with the biggest uphill elevation *gain* is Wedgemount Lake at 1,154 m.

Kilometers to Miles		Meters to Feet	
1 km	0.6 mi	100 m	328 ft
2 km	1.2 mi	200 m	656 ft
3 km	1.9 mi	300 m	984 ft
4 km	2.5 mi	400 m	1312 ft
5 km	3.1 mi	500 m	1640 ft
6 km	3.7 mi	600 m	1968 ft
7 km	4.3 mi	700 m	2296 ft
8 km	5.0 mi	800 m	2624 ft
9 km	5.6 mi	900 m	2952 ft
10 km	6.2 mi	1000 m	3280 ft
11 km	6.8 mi	1100 m	3608 ft
12 km	7.4 mi	1200 m	3936 ft
13 km	8.1 mi	1300 m	4264 ft
14 km	8.7 mi	1400 m	4592 ft
15 km	9.3 mi	1500 m	4920 ft
16 km	9.9 mi	1600 m	5248 ft
17 km	10.5 mi	1700 m	5576 ft
18 km	11.2 mi	1800 m	5904 ft
19 km	11.8 mi	1900 m	6232 ft
20 km	12.4 mi	2000 m	6560 ft
21 km	13.0 mi	2100 m	6880 ft
22 km	13.6 mi	2200 m	7216 ft
23 km	14.3 mi	2300 m	7544 ft
24 km	14.9 mi	2400 m	7872 ft
25 km	15.5 mi	2500 m	8200 ft
26 km	16.1 mi	2600 m	8528 ft
27 km	16.7 mi	2700 m	8856 ft
28 km	17.4 mi	2800 m	9184 ft

This is it!
eco-exhilaration™

ziptrek.com
604.935.0001
located inside the
Carleton Lodge across from
the Whistler Village Gondolas

WHISTLER CLIMATE

The springtime weather in Whistler can be a quick and intense affair with unsettled systems lasting until late June. In the summer there are two common weather patterns, both of which depend on the position of the jet stream, a fast flowing current of atmospheric air:

1. When the jet stream is north of the region, high pressure will usually dominate and bring clear skies and warm temperatures.

2. When the jet stream swings south, the Pacific disturbances can allow low-pressure systems to persist and bring rain and cooler temperatures.

In the summer, with the moderating affect of the Pacific Ocean, temperatures rarely climb to uncomfortable levels. A rotation of these systems will generally exist through early autumn. In October and November, the dreaded wet and grey conditions will usually settle upon the region.

For more information on the climate in Whistler, we recommend referring to Whistlerweather.org. This website is an excellent resource for the region's historical weather data as well as forecasts, webcams and satellite images.

Daylight	
Month	**Average / day**
March	11:00 hours
April	12:53 hours
May	14:36 hours
June	15:57 hours
July	16:10 hours
August	15:08 hours
September	13:28 hours
October	11:40 hours
November	9:52 hours

Table 1 *Average daily hours of light as measured in the Whistler valley for the months of March to November.*

Rainfall		
Month	**Average / month**	
March	50 mm	1.92 in
April	70 mm	2.76 in
May	80 mm	3.12 in
June	70 mm	2.76 in
July	50 mm	1.92 in
August	50 mm	1.92 in
September	70 mm	2.76 in
October	150 mm	5.88 in
November	120 mm	4.68 in

Table 2 *Average rainfall amounts (in millimeters and inches) as measured in the Whistler valley for the months of March to November.*

Damp day *A peaceful stroll along the Valley Trail in late season conditions.*

Table 3 *Average daily temperature high and low as measured in the Whistler valley for the months of March to November.*

Temperature				
Month	High	Low	High	Low
March	8 °C	-3 °C	46 °F	27 °F
April	11 °C	-2 °C	52 °F	36 °F
May	17 °C	7 °C	62 °F	44 °F
June	21 °C	9 °C	70 °F	48 °F
July	27 °C	11 °C	80 °F	52 °F
August	27 °C	11 °C	80 °F	52 °F
September	20 °C	8 °C	65 °F	46 °F
October	16 °C	3 °C	60 °F	38 °F
November	5 °C	-1 °C	41 °F	30 °F

Singing Pass Trail *Hikers returning from Russet Lake with dramatic glacial ice as a backdrop.*

CHAPTER 1:

WHISTLER HIKING TRAILS

Each spring, as the snow begins to melt away from North America's finest ski resort, an extensive network of hiking trails are revealed. This change in seasons brings with it the opportunity for a wide variety of walking opportunities. From casual strolls in the valley to exhilarating traverses in the high alpine, the motivated hiker in Whistler is never at a loss for a suitable outing.

The following chapter includes information on our favorite hikes, walks and trail runs in the area. These routes will afford you views of tumbling glaciers, jagged peaks, blankets of wildflowers and stands of massive ancient cedars. So get out there and enjoy the best hikes in Whistler. The adventure is right out your front door!

JUN YANAGISAWA

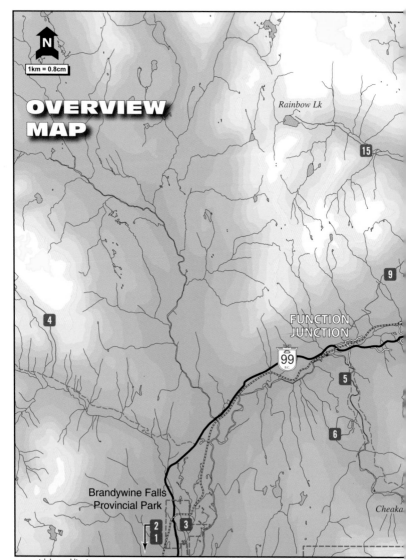

N

1km = 0.8cm

OVERVIEW MAP

Rainbow Lk

15

9

FUNCTION JUNCTION

99
B.C.

4

5

6

Brandywine Falls
Provincial Park

Cheaka

2
1

3

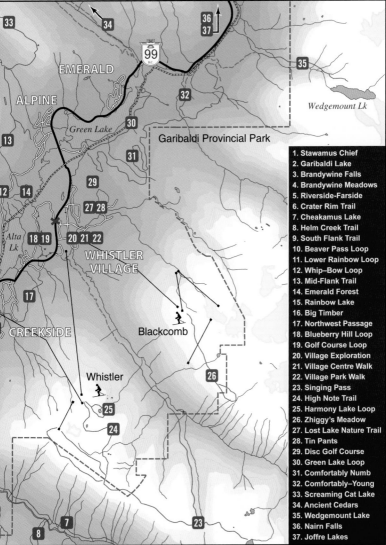

1. Stawamus Chief
2. Garibaldi Lake
3. Brandywine Falls
4. Brandywine Meadows
5. Riverside-Farside
6. Crater Rim Trail
7. Cheakamus Lake
8. Helm Creek Trail
9. South Flank Trail
10. Beaver Pass Loop
11. Lower Rainbow Loop
12. Whip–Bow Loop
13. Mid-Flank Trail
14. Emerald Forest
15. Rainbow Lake
16. Big Timber
17. Northwest Passage
18. Blueberry Hill Loop
19. Golf Course Loop
20. Village Exploration
21. Village Centre Walk
22. Village Park Walk
23. Singing Pass
24. High Note Trail
25. Harmony Lake Loop
26. Zhiggy's Meadow
27. Lost Lake Nature Trail
28. Tin Pants
29. Disc Golf Course
30. Green Lake Loop
31. Comfortably Numb
32. Comfortably–Young
33. Screaming Cat Lake
34. Ancient Cedars
35. Wedgemount Lake
36. Nairn Falls
37. Joffre Lakes

1 Stawamus Chief ★★★ . . . . ☐

STATS: 5.0km, 623m, February–December, N49 40.542 W123 09.194

Despite being 60 km south of Whistler, the Stawamus Chief is a highly recommended attraction for visitors. It's a world-famous rock climbing site and the sheer granite walls soar skyward for almost 600 m above the town of Squamish. It's a recreational paradise and the hikes are very popular, despite being steep and demanding. Awesome views of Howe Sound and Mt. Garibaldi can be seen from each of the three separate summits of the Chief.

The First Peak is the lowest, easiest and most popular summit and takes about 1–1.5 hours, one-way. It's a fine destination, but our favorite adventure avoids the First Peak in exchange for linking together the Second and Third. This route provides a more remote feel and gets you to the top of the highest point in the park, the Third Peak (702 m). This trail requires hikers to walk on sections of slippery rock and use chains and ladders fixed to the granite to assist their ascent. It should be considered an outing for experienced hikers and the summit sections are best avoided when wet. Save some energy for the descent! »

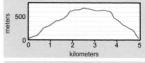

Access: *The trailhead is found at the south end of the Stawamus Chief Provincial Park campground.*

To Get There: *From Whistler, drive about 60 kilometers south on Highway 99 to Squamish. Zero your odometer at the intersection of Highway 99 and Cleveland Avenue (the intersection with the McDonalds). Continue driving south on Highway 99 and at 3.0 km turn left into Stawamus Chief Provincial Park. Park in any of the available lots. The closer you are to the campground (go right at the roundabout) the closer you are to the trailhead.*

Map: *Page 35*

Stawamus Chief *Clockwise from top right: The Stawamus Chief as seen from the Squamish estuary; view of Howe Sound from the First Peak; hungry critters on the summit; ladder climb to the Second Peak.*

Hiking: from the parking lots, walk through the campground and look for a BC Parks disclaimer sign beside a granite boulder. The sign states plainly that "This is NOT a walk in the park", and the mandatory scramble up the boulder to access the trail serves as an indication as to what lies ahead. Once up the boulder, follow the stairs as they climb steeply beside Oleson Creek. As the wooden stairs give way to a rugged trail of granite blocks and tree roots, start looking for signs directing you to the three separate summits of the Chief.

If you're up for an adventure, follow the signs to the Second Peak. The trail will eventually lead to steep, slippery granite slabs that have chains and a ladder permanently affixed to the rock to assist your climb. Look carefully for the orange, diamond-shaped markers on trees and orange paint on the rock. These blazes will lead you to the Second Peak and reward you with incredible views of Howe Sound and the Coast Mountains. After enjoying the panorama, you can either descend your approach route or carefully follow the orange paint and markers to the east. The markers, which are difficult to see in places, will lead you across the dome-shaped summit before descending to the top of the North Gully. From the top of the gully, the trail continues uphill and eventually follows granite ramps to the top of the Third Peak. For the descent, retrace your steps off the summit before descending through the forest back to the main trail.

Stawamus Chief *From top: View of Mt. Garibaldi from the Second Peak; the abundant plant Salal; bridge over Oleson Creek; tree fungus in old-growth forest.*

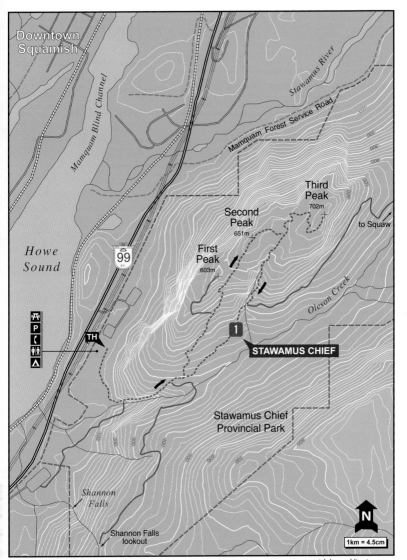

Downtown Squamish

Mamquam Blind Channel

Stawamus River

Mamquam Forest Service Road

Third Peak
702m

Second Peak
651m

to Squaw

First Peak
603m

Howe Sound

99

Oleson Creek

1

STAWAMUS CHIEF

Stawamus Chief Provincial Park

Shannon Falls

Shannon Falls lookout

N

1km = 4.5cm

2 Garibaldi Lake ★★★ . . . . ☐

STATS: 21.8km, 1067m, July–October, N49 57.449 W123 07.206

Garibaldi Lake is the crown jewel of Garibaldi Pro-vincial Park. It is a place of incredible beauty with an aquamarine lake framed by glaciated peaks on the east-ern shores. A beautifully maintained trail leads hikers elegantly uphill into this sublime alpine setting.

Hiking: From the parking lot, follow the trail as it switchbacks aggressively uphill under a canopy of massive Western red cedar and Douglas fir. Settle into a rhythm; you'll be gaining 810 meters of elevation! After 6.5 km, the incline of the trail takes on a more relaxed gradient. Look for the signs diverting you 100 meters off the main trail to the Barrier Viewpoint. This is a worthwhile side trip that provides views of the Barrier, a jumble of volcanic rock that is the *retaining* wall for the lakes above. After checking out the Barrier, return to the main trail and follow signs to Garibaldi Lake. ▸▸

Access: The trailhead is located 2.5 kilometers up Garibaldi Lake Road from Highway 99.

To Get There: Zero the odometer at the intersection of Highway 99 and Village Gate Boulevard and head south on Highway 99. At 24.5 km turn left onto Garib-aldi Lake Road. Bear right upon reaching an intersection with a yellow gate and at 27 km, arrive at the parking lot and trailhead (parking costs $3 as of 2008).

Map: Page 38

Garibaldi Lake *Clockwise from left: Battleship Islands; trail leading into the alpine; glacial ice suspended above the clear waters of Garibaldi Lake.*

On the way, you will pass two small lakes, Barrier Lake and Lesser Garibaldi Lake. Eventually, you will come to an intersection of trails above the massive Garibaldi Lake. Turn right at the intersection and walk down to the lake. The trail will take you across a small bridge and along the lakeshore to the campsite. The campsite is a worthy place to stop for a picnic or a break, but our favorite place to enjoy the view is from the Battleship Islands. There are two small peninsulas near the Battleships that you can walk out to. Both peninsulas offer log benches to sit upon, and the second one has a great view of Black Tusk. Please note that at some water levels, it may *not* be possible to walk out onto the peninsulas.

Descent: After enjoying the view at the lake, the most direct descent is to retrace your steps back to the parking lot. There is, however, a recommended diversion for parties with extra energy and time. This optional loop will take about an additional hour and will transport you into dramatic alpine meadows strewn with seasonal wildflowers.

Those interested in this option should walk 0.5 kilometers from the campsite back to the intersection of trails above the lake. Follow signs toward Black Tusk Viewpoint and climb through the forest and into the meadows. Walk along the trail through the meadows and turn left at the first intersection, following signs to Taylor Meadows. From here, the trail descends back to the main trail that you ascended at the start of the day and can be followed back to the parking lot.

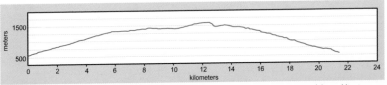

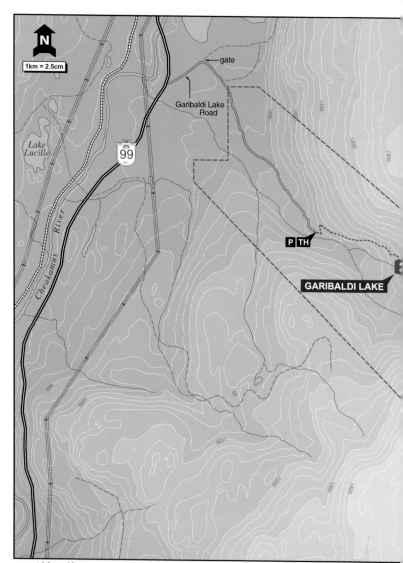

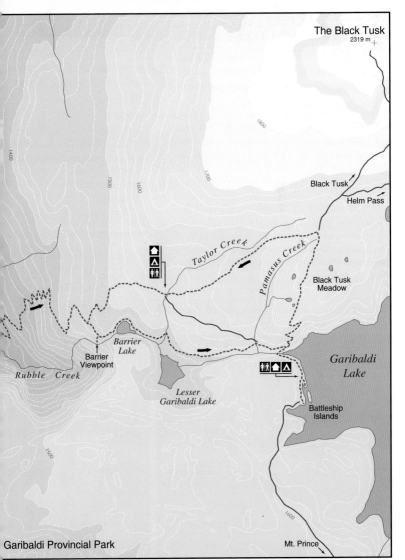

The Black Tusk
2319 m

Black Tusk

Helm Pass

Taylor Creek

Pamasus Creek

Black Tusk
Meadow

Barrier
Lake

Barrier
Viewpoint

Rubble Creek

Lesser
Garibaldi Lake

Garibaldi
Lake

Battleship
Islands

Garibaldi Provincial Park

Mt. Prince

3 Brandywine Falls Loop ★ . . . . ☐

STATS: 8.2km, 46m, May–October, N50 02.265 W123 07.249

Along this walk you will see several small lakes, a beautiful river, and a dramatic waterfall. The second half of the loop is much nicer than the first, so persevere!

Hiking: From the parking lot, locate the trailhead by the campsites. After a short walk, you will come to a T-junction. Turn left. (Going right would take you directly to the falls.) Follow the broad trail past small lakes and lily ponds until you reach a dirt road. Turn right and, staying on the road, walk through the whistle stop of McGuire Station (population: 1) to the railroad tracks. *Carefully* cross the tracks to a T-junction of trails. If you want to take a short side trip to the suspension bridge over the Callaghan Creek (just upstream of its confluence with the Cheakamus River), turn left. This is a recommended diversion on ▸▸

Access: *Start at the Brandywine Falls Provincial Park parking lot.*

To Get There: *Zero the odometer at the intersection of Highway 99 and Village Gate Boulevard and head south on Highway 99. At 16.9 km turn left into the Brandywine Falls Provincial Park parking lot.*

Map: *Page 45*

Brandywine Falls Loop *Counterclockwise from left: Suspension bridge over Callaghan Creek; Skunk Cabbage in spring; Brandywine Falls from the viewing platform.*

a really nice section of riverside trail. To continue the loop, turn right after crossing the tracks and walk along the singletrack through a beautiful forest back toward Brandywine Falls. Look for the optional trail heading into "Swim Lake," on your right, and check it out if you feel like a dip. Eventually, you will meet another T-junction. Turn left and walk 100 meters to the viewing platform near the falls. After enjoying the view, return to the parking lot.

Interesting Note: The name Brandywine Falls was derived from a 1910 bet over the height of the falls between Jack Nelson, chief of the Howe Sound and Northern survey party, and his axman, Bob Mollison. Nelson bet a bottle of brandy, Mollison a bottle of wine. A measuring chain was lowered over the falls, and the height was determined to be 70 meters. Mollison won the bet, and Nelson gave him the brandy—before christening the cascade Brandywine Falls.

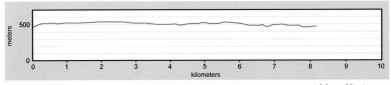

4 Brandywine Meadows ★ . . . . . ☐

STATS: 6.3km, 529m, July–October, N50 04.675 W123 11.135

Brandywine Meadows is most renowned for its concentration of wildflowers. And for good reason: The area is simply amazing in full bloom. Both the diversity and quantity of flowers in the meadow are incredible. The bad news is that the trail is in dire need of maintenance. It can be extremely muddy and in several places, trees have fallen across the path. That being said, it is still a worthy trip for parties who are willing to have a bit of an adventure. ▸▸

Access: The trailhead is located 6.6 kilometers up the Brandywine Creek Forest Service Road from Highway 99. Please note this a rugged dirt road. It has cavernous potholes and steep hills. It is not suitable for low-clearance vehicles.

To Get There: Zero the odometer at Highway 99 and Village Gate Boulevard and head south on Highway 99. At 14.1 km turn right onto the Brandywine Creek Forest Service Road. At 14.3 km go straight, avoiding the Brandywine West branch to the right. At 17.0 km go straight. At 18.6 km stay left at an intersection. At 18.7 km stay right at an intersection. At 20.0 km arrive at the bottom of the final steep hill before the trailhead. There are a couple of pull-offs below the hill at which you can park if your vehicle is not suited for climbing this incline. At 20.7 km reach the parking lot and trailhead, which is marked with a slender post.

Map: Page 44

Brandywine Meadows *This hike is one of Whistler's best for viewing wildflowers during the summer bloom.*

Hiking: From the trailhead, follow the trail as it climbs steeply uphill on the east side of the creek. As the incline becomes more gentle, the deep woods transition into alpine vegetation and vast meadows. Please realize that Brandywine Meadows is an extremely sensitive environment. Attempt to stay directly on the trail no matter how muddy it is as to avoid trampling the delicate alpine vegetation. After enjoying the meadows, return via the same route.

Note: A variety of unsanctioned variations to the lower trail have sprung up in an attempt to bypass some of the fallen trees. These routes are marked with flagging tape and are generally ill-advised. It is best to stick to the traditional route, designated with the orange diamond-shape markers on the trees.

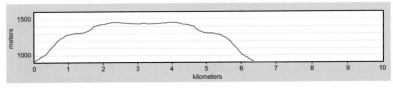

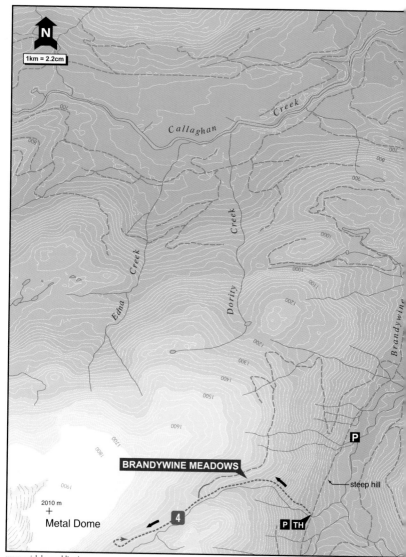

N

1km = 2.2cm

Callaghan Creek

Creek

Edna Creek

Dority Creek

Brandywine

BRANDYWINE MEADOWS

steep hill

P

P TH

4

2010 m
+
Metal Dome

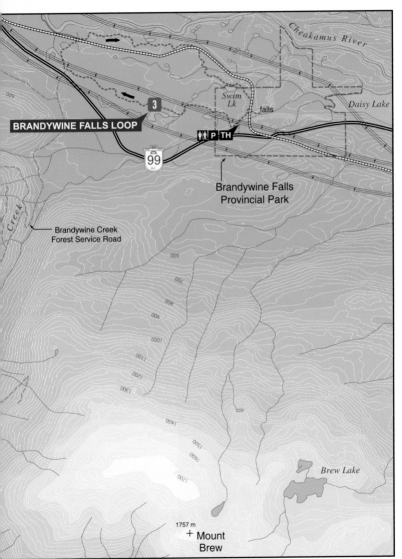

BRANDYWINE FALLS LOOP

3

99
BC

Swim
Lk

falls

Cheakamus River

Daisy Lake

Brandywine Falls
Provincial Park

Brandywine Creek
Forest Service Road

Creek

600

700

800

900

1000

1100

1200

1300

1400

1500

1600

1700

Brew Lake

1757 m
+ Mount
Brew

5 Riverside–Farside Loop ★★★ ☐

STATS: 4.8km, 104m, May–November, N50 04.868 W123 02.157

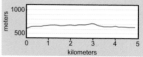

The Cheakamus River is simply a stunning natural feature. The river runs its course from Cheakamus Lake past steep rapids, through granite canyons, and over waterfalls to the confluence with the Squamish River north of Howe Sound. The Riverside–Farside Loop allows you to walk through the mossy forests beside the upper section of the river. The highlight, at the halfway point, is a crossing of the Cheakamus on a suspension bridge.

Hiking: From the trailhead, walk along the manicured trail upstream along the west bank of the Cheakamus River. There are a few deviations from the path (down to the river and up to the road), but it's pretty easy to stay on the main trail. Hike until you reach the suspension bridge and walk across it. As soon as crossing the bridge, look for the first trail on your left and take it, heading downstream. This is known as the Farside Trail. Avoid the spurs leading to the right and up to the Cheakamus Lake Road. Staying on the trail will eventually deposit you back at the bridge near where you started. Cross the bridge on the sidewalk and return to your vehicle.

Access: The signed trailhead is located off Westside Main road, near the south side of the bridge over the Cheakamus River.

To Get There: Zero the odometer at Highway 99 and Village Gate Boulevard. Drive south and at 7.3 km turn left onto Cheakamus Lake Road. At 7.8 km stay right (on the pavement) at an intersection with a dirt road and drive across the bridge over the Cheakamus River. At 7.9 km the Riverside trailhead is on your left after crossing the bridge. At 8.0 km turn left onto the dirt road known as Westside Main (be careful as this is a bit of a blind turn and it's difficult to see vehicles travelling in the opposite direction). Park in the dirt lot on the left. *Note:* This acccess may change slightly due to construction.

Map: Page 48

Riverside–Farside Loop *The Cheakamus River is a dramatic waterway and the suspension bridge provides a great view.*

6 Crater Rim Trail ★★ . . . . ☐

STATS: 4.3km, 221m, June–October, N50 03.803 W123 01.996

This is a great, rugged trail that circumnavigates the rim of an ancient volcanic cone. Geologists believe that a volcano rose out of the glacial ice at this site about 10,000 years ago. As the lava cooled, it created the columnar basalt rock formations that are visible on the slopes above Loggers Lake. The lake lies in the remnant volcanic crater.

Hiking: This hike starts at an old logging road that is well-marked with a map and sign to Loggers Lake. Walk up the steep, rocky logging road for about 250 meters to the Crater Rim trailhead on your left. Take this trail as it leads up to an overlook above Loggers Lake. After enjoying the view, continue up the rocky trail designated with orange markers on the trees, avoiding the signed trail leading down to Basalt Valley. Continue hiking along the trail as it traverses high above the west shores of Loggers Lake. Eventually, the trail will lead you down a series of switchbacks to a junction with the broad Ridge Trail. Turn right onto the trail and follow it back to Loggers Lake. It will lead you around the north end of the lake and back to the Crater Rim trailhead. Descend to your car.

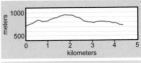

Access: The trailhead is located off Westside Main road, a couple of kilometers beyond the bridge over the Cheakamus River.

To Get There: Zero the odometer at Highway 99 and Village Gate Boulevard. Drive south and at 7.3 km turn left onto Cheakamus Lake Road. At 7.8 km stay right (on the pavement) at an intersection with a dirt road and drive across the Cheakamus River bridge. At 8.0 km turn left onto the dirt road known as Westside Main (be careful as this is a bit of a blind turn and it's difficult to see vehicles travelling in the opposite direction). At 10.1 km park in the dirt lot on the left. The trail starts on the other side of the road.

Map: Page 49

Crater Rim Trail *View of Logger's Lake from above. The basalt debris on the background slope is part of the volcanic cone.*

Cheakamus Lk Rd

FARSIDE

5

RIVERSIDE

P

TH

Function
Junction

99

Olympic
Village
[changes likely]

Ridge
Trail

Cheakamus River

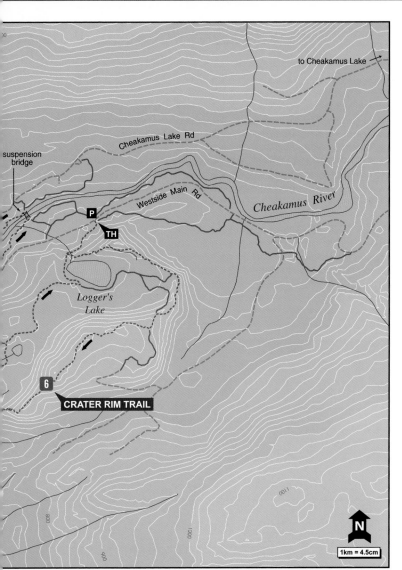

to Cheakamus Lake

Cheakamus Lake Rd

suspension bridge

Westside Main Rd

Cheakamus River

P

TH

Logger's Lake

6

CRATER RIM TRAIL

N

1km = 4.5cm

7 Cheakamus Lake ★★★ . . . . . . ☐

STATS: 14.5km, 49m, June–October, N50 02.515 W122 59.368

This deservedly popular walk requires no elevation gain and accesses the magnificent Cheakamus Lake. The trail leads past granite outcrops and humbling stands of massive, ancient cedars and Douglas fir. It is truly a special place. Many visitors turn around once reaching the lake (approximately 1.5 hours return time), but it is well worth walking to the end of the maintained trail where Singing Creek drains into the lake (approximately 3.5 hours return time). There is a small rocky beach at this point that makes a great lunch spot. Enjoy!

Hiking: Locate the trailhead at the east end of the parking lot. Follow the trail through the spectacular forest for 3 kilometers to the outlet of the river from the lake. The trail continues from here, along the north shore of the lake, for another 4 kilometers to Singing Creek. Return via the same route.

Cheakamus Lake Access: The trail starts at the Cheakamus Lake parking lot, 7 kilometers up the Cheakamus Lake Road.

To Get There: Zero the odometer at the intersection of Highway 99 and Village Gate Boulevard and head south on Highway 99. At 7.3 km turn left onto Cheakamus Lake Road, opposite Function Junction. At 7.8 km turn left, leaving the pavement, as directed by the signs to Cheakamus Lake. At 14.6 km Cheakamus Lake Road ends at the parking lot.

Map: Page 55

Cheakamus Lake *Clockwise from left: Bridge to Helm Campground over the Cheakamus River; view down the length of Cheakamus lake; gorgeous trail through old-growth forest.*

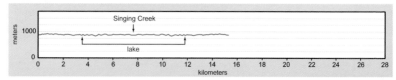

8 Helm Creek Trail ★★ . . . . ☐

STATS: 25.6km, 958m, July–October, N50 02.521 W122 59.382

The Helm Creek Trail provides access to the meadows and Cinder Flats beneath Black Tusk. The trail is very well-maintained, and although it gains a significant amount of vertical, it is less demanding than the trail to Wedgemount Lake. The real treat of this trip is popping out of the forest onto the meadows surrounding Helm Campground, with the stunning views of Black Tusk above.

> **Helm Creek Trail Access:** Same as Cheakamus Lake.
>
> **Map:** Page 54

Hiking: From the parking lot, follow the trail toward Cheakamus Lake for 1.5 kilometers. At this point, you will see a well-marked junction of trails. Turn right and follow the trail down to the sturdy, metal footbridge over the Cheakamus River. Walk across the bridge and begin climbing up the gradual switchbacks that traverse the steep terrain on the east side of Helm Creek. The trail transitions into more gradual terrain with sub-alpine vegetation and glimpses of the creek below. It eventually deposits hikers in a dramatic fashion onto the meadows of Helm Campground below Black Tusk. From here, retrace your route back to Cheakamus Lake parking lot.

▸▸

Note Although Helm Campground is a fine objective, parties with sufficient time and energy can continue walking up the trail through the meadows. After about 3.5 kilometers of walking, the lush meadows will give way to the barren Cinder Flats beneath the Black Tusk. The Flats are an expanse of volcanic rock that hold a couple of small lakes, one of them being Helm Lake. The area has very little vegetation and is quite unique. Beyond the Cinder Flats are the switchbacks that lead up to Helm Pass (another 2 km). The views of the Tantalus Range from just past Helm Pass are simply stunning in fine weather, but this added walk makes for an extremely long day from the trailhead. As always, remember to set a turnaround time, allowing for daylight and energy to return to your vehicle at the Cheakamus Lake parking lot!

Helm Creek Trail *From left: Hikers relax in the beautiful Helm Campground meadows with stunning views toward the Black Tusk; directions through the volcanic landscape leading back from Helm Pass.*

Interesting Fact: the native people referred to the Black Tusk as nq'il'qtens ku skenknap or "seat of thunder". It was said to be the perch for the legendary Thunder Bird and the black rock was said to have been charred by lightning!

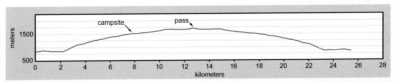

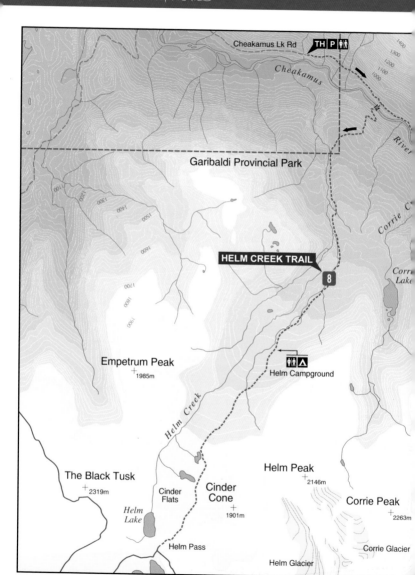

Cheakamus Lk Rd **TH** **P**

Cheakamus

River

Garibaldi Provincial Park

Corrie C

HELM CREEK TRAIL **8**

Corr
Lake

Empetrum Peak
+1985m

Helm Campground

Helm Creek

The Black Tusk
+2319m

Cinder
Flats

Cinder
Cone
+1901m

Helm Peak
+2146m

Helm
Lake

Corrie Peak
+2263m

Helm Pass

Helm Glacier

Corrie Glacier

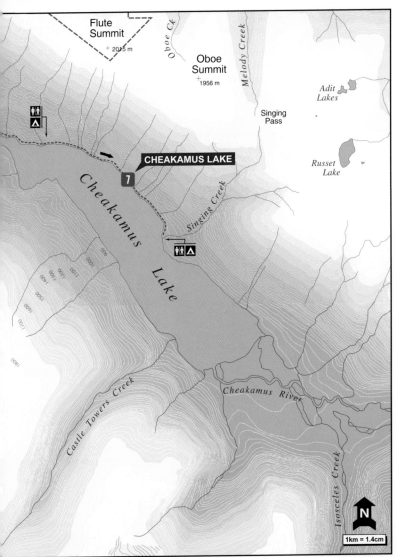

Flute
Summit
+ 2015 m

O b o e   C k

Oboe
Summit
+ 1956 m

Melody Creek

Singing
Pass

Adit
Lakes

Russet
Lake

CHEAKAMUS LAKE

7

Cheakamus

Singing Creek

Lake

900
1000
1100
1200
1300
1400
1500
1600
1700

1800

Castle Towers Creek

Cheakamus River

Isosceles Creek

N

1km = 1.4cm

9 South Flank Trail ★★ . . . . □

STATS: 7.9km, 525m, June–October, N50 05.345 W123 02.411

This section of the Flank starts in Function Junction and traverses the southeast slope of Sproatt Mountain, finishing at the Rainbow Trail trailhead. It provides awesome views of the iconic peaks in the area: Black Tusk, Whistler, Blackcomb, Fissile, Fitzsimmons, Wedge, Mt. Currie, and Rainbow. The views at the north end of the trail display the entire Whistler valley with Alta Lake in the foreground and both ski areas behind.   ▸▸

Access: The trail starts where Miller Creek flows under Alpha Lake Road in Function Junction. The trailhead is signed and found near the intersection of Alpha Lake Road and Miller Creek Road.

To Get to the Start: Zero the odometer at the intersection of Highway 99 and Village Gate Boulevard and head south on Highway 99. At 7.3 km turn right onto Alpha Lake Road. At 7.5 km the Flank trailhead is on the left. Park here.

To Get to the End: Zero the odometer at the intersection of Highway 99 and Village Gate Boulevard and drive north. At 3.8 km turn left at the traffic lights onto Alpine Way. At 3.9 km turn left at the stop sign onto Rainbow Drive. At 5.0 km Rainbow Drive turns into Alta Lake Road. At 6.8 km turn right into the Rainbow Trail parking lot.

Map: Page 61

Flank Trail *The user-friendly Flank Trail accommodates hikers as well as mountain bikers.*

Flank Trail *From top: Forest mushroom in fall; view of Wedge Mountain; one of the many Flank Trail directional signs.*

Hiking: Locate the trailhead in Function Junction and walk into the forest. Stay right at two ensuing trail junctions, following signs toward "Rainbow." Soon the trail will start to climb to an elevation of just over 1,000 meters and provide rewarding views of Black Tusk and Whistler Mountain. The trail hovers around this elevation for a couple of kilometers before descending gradually to an intersection with the dirt road that leads to the Upper Rainbow Trail. Turn right (downhill) onto this road. Stay on the road, below the small building with the blue metal roof (the Twenty-one Mile Creek filtration building) to a T-junction of roads. Immediately across the road from the T-junction, the Lower Rainbow Trail begins and leads downhill to the Rainbow Trail parking lot on Alta Lake Road and the end of this section of the Flank Trail.

Note: Since you finish this trail a long distance from the start, it is best arrange some sort of a car shuttle or drop-off. Trust us, it's worth the hassle!

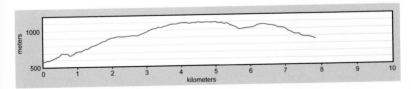

10 Beaver Pass Loop ★ . . . . ☐

STATS: 1.4km, 22m, May–October, N50 06.736 W122 59.798

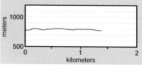

Enjoy a unique perspective of Whistler Mountain from a hike within one of the most exclusive housing developments in town.

Hiking: The trailhead is marked with a large stone obelisk that reads "Beaver Pass." Head up the dirt road with the yellow gate across it. The road will bend to the left and bring you above a small lake studded with dead trees. Keep walking past the lake and start looking for the first singletrack (known as Beaver Pond Trail) leading into the forest on your left. The singletrack is marked with a small sign and located at the bottom of a short downhill section. Turn left onto the singletrack. The trail will wrap back around the lake and return you to Stonebridge Drive. From here, you can walk back across the bridge over Scotia Creek to your car.

Access: *This trail starts on the west side of Stonebridge Drive near the bridge over Scotia Creek.*

To Get There: *Zero your odometer at the intersection of Highway 99 and Village Gate Boulevard Head south on Highway 99. At 5.1 km turn right onto Alta Lake Rd. At 7.4 km turn left, through the stone obelisks, onto Stonebridge Drive. At 8.7 km the trailhead will be on your left. Park on the shoulder of Stonebridge Drive.*

Map: *Page 60*

Beaver Pass Loop *From left: A very elaborate sign post marks the trailhead; view of the beaver pond with mountain reflection.*

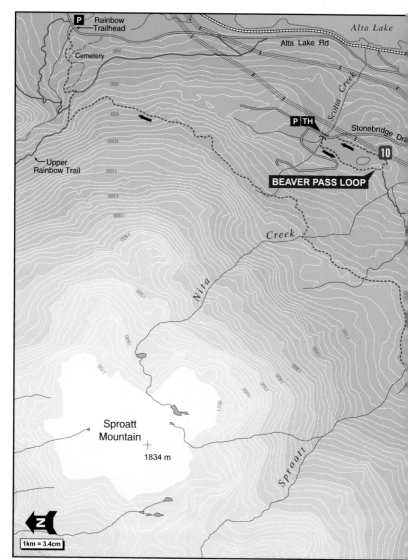

Rainbow Trailhead

Cemetery

Upper Rainbow Trail

Alta Lake

Alta Lake Rd

Scotia Creek

Stonebridge Dr

BEAVER PASS LOOP

10

Nita Creek

Sproatt

Sproatt Mountain
1834 m

1km = 3.4cm

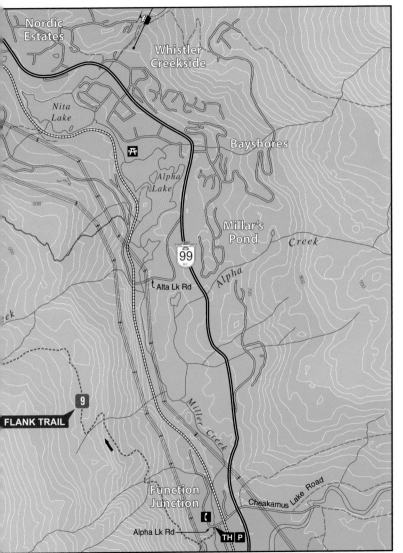

Nordic
Estates

Whistler
Creekside

Nita
Lake

Bayshores

Alpha
Lake

Millar's
Pond

Creek

99
B.C.

Alta Lk Rd

Alpha

FLANK TRAIL   9

Miller Creek

Function
Junction

Cheakamus Lake Road

Alpha Lk Rd

TH P

11 Lower Rainbow Loop ★★ . . . . ☐

STATS: 2.3km, 114m, May–October, N50 07.809 W122 59.141

This is a recommended loop with the option to check out a pretty waterfall.

Hiking: Start up the Rainbow Trail on the west side of Twenty-one Mile Creek. The trail ascends through the forest, at one point paralleling a dirt road. Look for the signposted trail on your right, directing you to Rainbow Falls. The short trip down to the falls is optional, but we highly recommend it! After visiting the falls, retrace your steps back to the main Rainbow Trail. Continue walking uphill until you meet a dirt road at the site of the Twenty-one Mile Creek filtration building. Join the road and stay right (between the building and the creek). Look for the trail on your right, leading down to a wooden footbridge across Twenty-one Mile Creek. Take this trail and cross the bridge. Follow it for a brief climb past the junction with the Flank Trail and then a steady descent back to the Rainbow Trail parking lot.

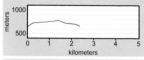

Access: Start at the Rainbow Trail parking lot.

To Get To There: Zero the odometer at Highway 99 and Village Gate Blvd. and drive north. At 3.8 km turn left onto Alpine Way. At 3.9 km turn left onto Rainbow Drive, which becomes Alta Lake Road. At 6.8 km turn right into the Rainbow Trail parking lot.

Map: Page 69

12 Whip–Bow Loop ★★ . . . . ☐

STATS: 4.3km, 147m, May–October, N50 07.184 W122 59.186

This loop is a fusion of Whip Me Snip Me and the Lower Rainbow Loop. It's a fantastic trail run with a gradual ascent and a firm, switchback descent.

Hiking: From the parking lot, walk south on Alta Lake Road to the well-marked Whip Me Snip Me trailhead (80m). Hike up the wide, rocky trail, passing under the power lines. Turn right at a junction of two wide trails and climb gradually until you meet a dirt road near a small building with a blue metal roof. Descend the road below the building until you can turn left onto another dirt road, immediately past the building. Shortly, look for a trail on the right, leading down to a wooden footbridge across Twenty-one Mile Creek. Once across the creek, check out the waterfall and canyon that are visible through the trees! Walk past a junction with the Flank Trail and descend back down to Alta Lake Road. Walk 1 km back to the car.

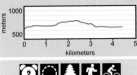

Access: Start at the Rainbow Park parking lot.

To Get There: Zero the odometer at the intersection of Highway 99 and Village Gate Boulevard and head north on Highway 99. At 3.8 km turn left at the traffic lights onto Alpine Way. At 3.9 km turn left at the stop sign onto Rainbow Drive. At 5.0 km Rainbow Drive turns into Alta Lake Road. At 7.9 km turn left into the Rainbow Park parking lot.

Map: Page 69

Lower Rainbow Falls *From left: Rainbow Falls is a scenic spot that is very accessible; admiring the water from the bridge; pointing the way to Whip Me Snip Me.*

13 Mid-Flank Trail ★★★ . . . . ☐

STATS: 22.4km, 443m, June–October, N50 07.815 W122 59.096

This section of the Flank Trail starts at the Rainbow Trail trailhead and finishes in the subdivision of Alpine Meadows. It is hard to overstate the amazing views that reward hikers walking on this section of the Flank Trail. Like the stretch from Function Junction to the Rainbow trailhead, all of the iconic peaks of the area (with the exception of Rainbow) can be seen in panoramic splendor along the way. The views from Whistler Mountain north to Mount Currie, inclusive of Whistler Village and Green Lake at the paragliding launch site above Alpine Meadows, are among the finest in the corridor. Save it for a bluebird day!

Note: Unlike the other sections of the Flank, you can make a nice loop out of this trail, although you have to walk beside Alta Lake Road for a spell. The loop is described below. Alternatively, arrange a car shuttle.

Hiking: From the parking lot, find the Flank Trail trailhead on the east side of Twenty-one Mile Creek. After gaining 50 meters of elevation on the trail, you will reach the intersection with Bob's Rebob. Stay left at this intersection, walk through the wooden chicane and gain a further 70 meters of elevation to another trail junction. Turn left and prepare for the notorious "27 Switchbacks"! After the switchbacks, stay left at a trail junction and continue the ascent to an elevation above 1,100 meters. After reaching this elevation, you will soon come across the site where many famous images showing Whistler and Blackcomb in their panoramic splendor are taken. Continue along the broad Flank Trail to the paragliding launch site, recognizable as the clear area with a windsock mounted in the trees above. This is a prime picnic spot and another great photo opportunity! After enjoying the view, continue along the Flank through another chicane and the junction with the rocky road known as Rick's Roost. ▶▶

Access: Start at the Rainbow Trail parking lot.

To Get to the Start: Use the same directions as for Lower Rainbow Loop.

To Get to the End: Zero the odometer at the intersection of Highway 99 and Village Gate Blvd. Start off driving north on the highway. At 3.8 km turn left onto Alpine Way at the traffic lights. At 4.8 km Alpine Way ends in a cul-de-sac. Turn around in the cul-de-sac and find a legal parking spot on Alpine Way.

Map: Page 68

Added Value: When descending the rocky road known as Rick's Roost, look carefully for the sign that states this name on the left. Take the time to walk along the short path below the sign to a park bench at a viewpoint. This is another great opportunity to enjoy the panoramic alpine views!

Winter Light *View of Blackcomb Mountain from the Flank Trail in splendid winter conditions.*

Turn right and descend the road until it joins the end of the paved Alpine Way in the Alpine Meadows subdivision. Pick up your car or...

If you are continuing on foot back to the Rainbow Trail trailhead, here is our favorite route: Follow Alpine Way to your second right onto Fissile Lane, followed by your next right onto Forest Ridge Drive. Walk to the end of Forest Ridge and locate the start of Mel's Dilemma trail (defined by a little bridge) at the edge of the forest. Follow the most-defined of the myriad of trails in this area down to Alta Lake Road. Cross the road at the crosswalk and walk along the shoulder of Alta Lake Road for about 1.5 kilometers until you see the well-marked trailhead for Bart's Dark on the left. (You will see a trail to the left before Bart's Dark, but it is a technical mountain bike trail known as A River Runs Through It and is not great for walking.) Turn onto Bart's and follow the double track into the forest. Stay right and you will end up at the dirt parking lot directly across from the Rainbow Trail trailhead. From here, you can cross Alta Lake Road at the crosswalk to your car.

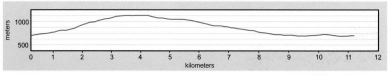

14 Emerald Forest ★ . . . . ☐

STATS: 2.8km, 51m, May–October, N50 07.632 W122 58.267

The Emerald Forest Conservation Area is a 56-hectare expanse of old-growth forest and wetland that houses over 250 plant and animal species. One of these species is the striking, green moss that earned the area its name. The Emerald Forest was preserved in February 2000 in recognition that it is a critical natural corridor linking Alta Lake with Green Lake to the north. There are many hiking variations within the area and our favorite is described below.

Hiking: From the end of Lorimer Road, locate the paved Valley Trail and follow it to the right (north). Walk over the pedestrian bridge spanning the River of Golden Dreams and cautiously cross the railroad tracks. Locate the three interpretive signs on the border of the Emerald Forest. From the signs, follow the wide path uphill beside an overgrown gravel pit for a short distance until you see an unmarked trail. Take the trail up to the top of the gravel pit and follow it into the forest. While walking in the forest, you will come upon four successive trail junctions. Stay right

▶▶

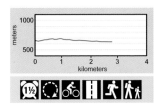

Access: *Park and start hiking at the end of Lorimer Road.*

To Get There: *Zero the odometer at the intersection of Highway 99 and Village Gate Boulevard. Start off driving north on the highway. At 0.6 km turn left onto Lorimer Road. At 1.9 km arrive at small parking area at the end of Lorimer Road. It also possible to walk here from the Village on the Valley Trail.*

Map: *Page 69*

Emerald Forest *From left: Green moss-covered boulders frame the forest trail; enjoying views to the north from the observation platform.*

at the first, left at the second, right at the third, and left at the fourth. From the fourth trail junction, follow the trail until it joins the paved Valley Trail. Turn right onto the Valley Trail and follow it downhill. Before reaching a T-junction, look for a wide gravel trail heading gradually uphill on your right. Follow it to a wooden observation platform on which you can enjoy panoramic views from Mt. Currie to Blackcomb with the protected wetlands in the foreground. From the platform, walk down the steps to the Valley Trail and turn right. From here, the trail will take you back to the end of Lorimer Road.

Interesting Fact: The Emerald Forest has an industrious history. As part of the Pemberton Trail, it was an important trade route for the indigenous people and, much later, European fur traders. In 1913, the Pacific Great Eastern Railway began construction to allow for the train traffic that continues to this day through the area. The '50s and '60s saw selective logging in the area, and gravel was mined from the pits on the south end of the area as recently as the 1980s.

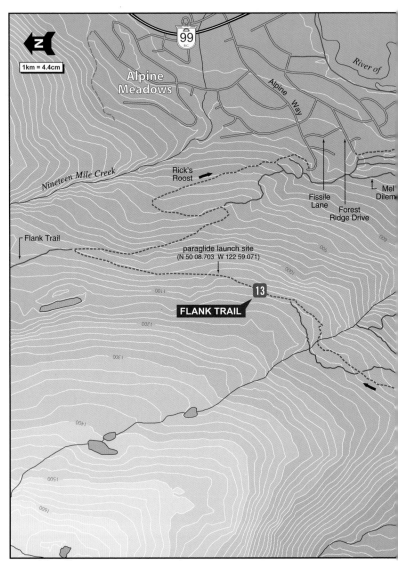

1km = 4.4cm

Alpine Meadows

River of

Alpine Way

Nineteen Mile Creek

Rick's Roost

Fissile Lane

Forest Ridge Drive

Mel Dilem

Flank Trail

paraglide launch site
(N 50 08.703 W 122 59.071)

900

700

1000

13

FLANK TRAIL

1100

1200

1300

1400

1500

1600

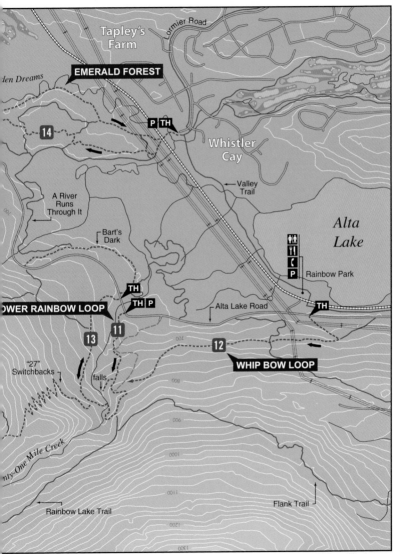

Tapley's
Farm

Cormier Road

EMERALD FOREST

len Dreams

14

P TH

Whistler
Cay

← Valley
Trail

*Alta
Lake*

A River
Runs
Through It

Bart's
Dark

Rainbow Park
P

TH
TH P

OWER RAINBOW LOOP

Alta Lake Road →
TH

"27"
Switchbacks

13

11

700

12

WHIP BOW LOOP

falls

800

006

nty-One Mile Creek

0001

Rainbow Lake Trail

0011

Flank Trail →

0021

1300

15 Rainbow Lake ★★★ . . . . ☐

STATS: 18.4km, 888m, July–October, N50 07.803 W122 59.142

For years, you've looked across the valley at Rainbow Mountain while skiing at Whistler and Blackcomb. Now, it's time to go check it out.

Hiking: Start up the Rainbow Trail on the south side of Twenty-one Mile Creek. The trail ascends through the forest, at one point paralleling a dirt road. Continue walking uphill on the trail until you meet a dirt road at the site of the Twenty-one Mile Creek filtration building. At this point, walk on the road underneath the building and follow the road as it turns uphill to the right. Stay on the road, passing the trailheads for Whip Me Snip Me and the Flank Trail until the road turns to singletrack and enters the old-growth forest. You will cross a few boardwalks over marshy ground and bridges over tributaries feeding Twenty-one Mile Creek. On the final set of switchbacks, look for a smooth rocky outcrop providing dramatic views of Wedge and Blackcomb mountains. After taking the obligatory photo, make the final push up to Rainbow Lake.

If you're not too weary, the best views and wildflowers can be seen on the hike to Rainbow Pass; the height of land above and beyond the west shore of the lake. Once at the pass, you can look down to Hanging Lake and across to the striking Pemberton Icecap. It's a great place for lunch! Retrace your route to get back to the car.

Access: Start at the Rainbow Trail parking lot.

To Get To There: Zero the odometer at the intersection of Highway 99 and Village Gate Boulevard and head north on Highway 99. At 3.8 km turn left at the traffic lights onto Alpine Way. At 3.9 km turn left at the stop sign onto Rainbow Drive. At 5.0 km Rainbow Drive turns into Alta Lake Road. At 6.8 km turn right into the Rainbow Trail parking lot.

Map: Page 73

Rainbow Lake *This alpine pool is the main source of Whistler's drinking water.*

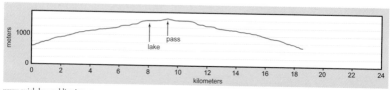

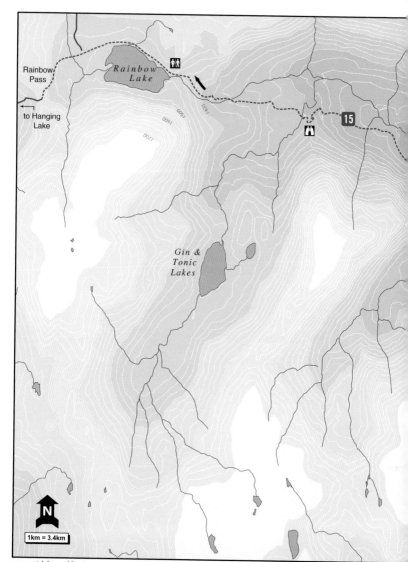

Rainbow Pass

Rainbow Lake

to Hanging Lake

15

Gin & Tonic Lakes

N

1km = 3.4km

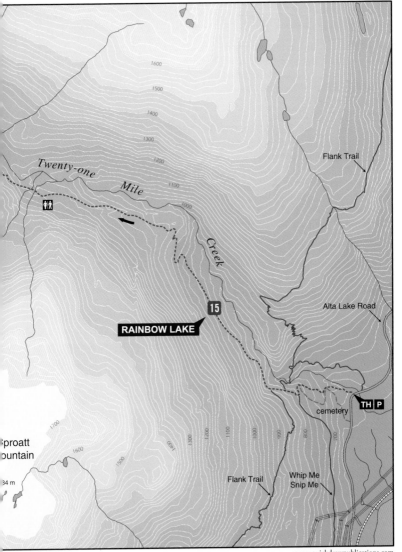

Twenty-one Mile Creek

1600
1500
1400
1300
1200
1100
1000

Flank Trail

15

RAINBOW LAKE

Alta Lake Road

TH P

cemetery

Sproatt
Mountain

34 m

1700
1600
1500
1400
1300
1200
1100
1000
900
800
700

Flank Trail

Whip Me
Snip Me

16 Big Timber ★ . . . . ☐

STATS: 2.8km, 189m, May–October, N50 07.469 W122 57.703

This walk through the "big timber" provides nice views of Mt. Tricouni, Rainbow Mountain and Mt. Currie. The loop climbs a singletrack through the forest before descending a dirt road back to the start.

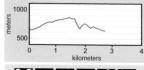

Hiking – From London Lane, start walking along the double-track trail on the south side of Whistler Creek (the same side of the creek as the Legends Hotel). This trail will lead uphill, beside the ski run (Lower Dave Murray Downhill). Walk until you see a wooden bridge on your left. From the wooden bridge, look directly across the ski run and locate the snowmaking tower and Tower No. 2 of the Creekside Gondola. Walk across the ski run and locate the start of Big Timber Trail, just uphill of the snowmaking tower.

The trail leads above Tower 2 of the gondola and across another ski run (Lower Peak to Creek) before starting a steady climb. Continue uphill until you get to a junction of trails above a wooden viewing platform. Continue in the same direction (as opposed to heading uphill on the trail to your right) after stepping down to the platform for the great view. A short walk from the platform leads to a set of stairs and a second viewing deck, providing great views of Alta Lake and Mt. Currie to the north. From this deck, continue walking along the trail until you get deposited onto a dirt road. Turn left and descend the road back to where you started.

Access: Start the loop on the south side of Whistler Creek at a point where the creek flows into a culvert under London Lane.

To Get There: Zero the odometer at the intersection of Highway 99 and Village Gate Boulevard and head south on Highway 99. At 3.6 km turn left onto London Lane. At 3.8 km the trailhead will be on your left. Park in the lot on your right.

Map: Page 77

Big Timber *Left to right: A mountain biker rolls by the observation platform on Big Timber; a massive Douglas fir pushes skyward.*

17 Northwest Passage Loop ★ . . ☐

STATS: 8.2km, 276m, June–October, N50 05.715 W122 59.360

This loop starts at Creekside and takes the Northwest Passage to Brio before crossing the highway and returning via the Valley Trail. It's a great workout!

Access: Same as Big Timber.

Hiking: From the point where Whistler Creek flows under London Lane, start walking uphill along the double track on the south side of the creek (the same side of the creek as Legends Hotel). This trail will lead you up the side of a ski run known as the Lower Dave Murray Downhill. Continue uphill (passing the wooden footbridge on your left) and look carefully for the point where Whistler Creek flows under the ski run. At this point, a dirt road leads into the forest on your left. Walk onto the dirt road and follow it, avoiding two intersecting dirt roads, until you meet the paved road, Nordic Way.

Walk uphill beside Nordic Way until you see At Nature's Door condominiums. Walk through the gate and immediately look for a gravel road on your left. Follow it as it winds uphill past a wooden observation platform, eventually joining the Lower Dave Murray Downhill. Once back on the ski run, walk directly uphill for a short distance and turn left onto an overgrown road, known as the Northwest Passage. Follow it under a small cliff, which is at the same elevation as Tower 12 (if you are unsure, walk over to the lift line and verify that you are in the right spot).

The Northwest Passage traverses the northwest flank of Whistler Mountain before steadily descending. At the end of the descent, you will cross a crude bridge over a small creek. Immediately after crossing the creek, look for a singletrack heading into the forest on your left. At this point, leave the Northwest Passage and take the singletrack into the forest. Once on the singletrack, stay right at a junction of trails and follow it to the paved road, Panorama Ridge, in the subdivision of Brio. Turn right onto Panorama Ridge, followed by a left onto Arbutus Drive and a right onto Brio Entrance. Follow Brio Entrance to Highway 99. Walk south along the shoulder of Highway 99 for a short distance to the traffic lights at Blueberry Drive and cross the highway at the crosswalk. After crossing the highway, join the Valley Trail and follow it back to the parking lot at Creekside.

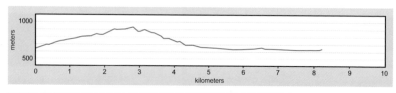

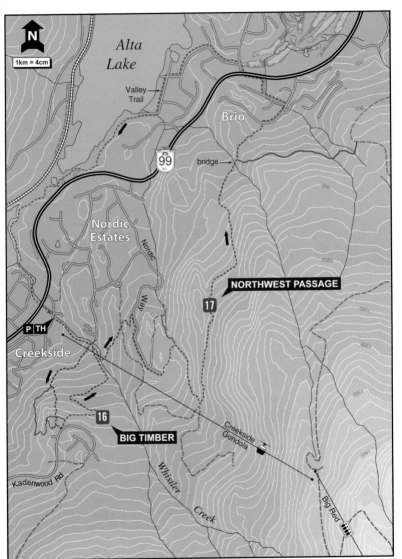

18 Blueberry Hill Loop ★★ . . . . . ☐

STATS: 4.1km, 82m, May–October, N50 06.760 W122 58.492

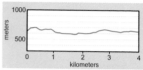

This is an extremely varied loop incorporating the narrow Blueberry Trail above Alta Lake and the paved Valley Trail next to the Whistler Golf Club. It provides a great opportunity to familiarize yourself with the geography of the area and has incredible views of Alta Lake, Rainbow Mountain, Sproatt Mountain, Blackcomb Mountain, and Whistler Mountain. It also lets you look at the multi-million dollar homes overlooking the golf course!

Hiking: The trail starts climbing immediately. After a traverse through the forest, descend steeply down to a junction with a broad path. Turn right and follow the path for a short distance looking for a little footbridge on your left. Walk across the bridge into a small clearing and then into a stand of trees. Once through the trees, you will meet Crabapple Drive. Walk beside Crabapple Drive until it is intersected by the paved Valley Trail at a raised crosswalk. Turn right onto the Valley Trail and follow it a short distance to a point where the trail splits. Turn right and continue walking on the Valley Trail beside the golf course. It will eventually lead you to the intersection of Blueberry Drive and St. Anton Way.

Access: Start at the Blueberry Trail trailhead on St. Anton Way in the Alta Vista subdivision.

To Get There: Zero the odometer at the intersection of Highway 99 and Village Gate Boulevard and head south on Highway 99. At 1.2 km turn right onto Blueberry Drive. At 1.3 km turn left onto St. Anton Way. At 1.5 km curve right, staying on St. Anton Way. At 1.7 km Blueberry Trail trailhead is on your right.

Note: There is limited roadside parking near the trailhead. If possible, walk to the trailhead via the Valley Trail.

Map: Page 81

Blueberry Hill Loop *From left: Trailhead marker; strolling along the Valley Trail adjacent to the picturesque Whistler Golf Club.*

19 Whistler Golf Club Loop ★★★ ☐

STATS: 4.6km, 57m, Year-round, N50 06.872 W122 57.623

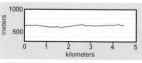

This is a nice stroll from the village, with great views of both ski hills and lots of homes that we wish we could afford! This is also a fantastic running route for those staying in the village.

Hiking: Locate the paved Valley Trail near the golf course clubhouse. From here, the only directions you should need are "stay on the Valley Trail and keep left." Your goal is to circumnavigate the golf course. The Valley Trail will bring you back to the clubhouse at the end of the loop.

Access: The trail starts near the Whistler Golf Club clubhouse.

To Get To There: Start in Village Square, in the heart of Whistler Village. Walk along Golfers Approach (between the Liquor Store and Citta') until a ramp or stairs brings you to the paved Whistler Way. Cross Whistler Way and walk on the sidewalk toward Highway 99. Take your first left, and walk through the tunnel under the highway to the clubhouse.

Map: Page 81 and 90

Interesting Fact: The Whistler Golf Club is an Arnold Palmer-designed course. Currently, there are three golf courses in town, with the Whistler Golf Club being the original.

Whistler Golf Club Loop *Golf aficionados enjoy lush fairways amidst gorgeous mountain valley homes.*

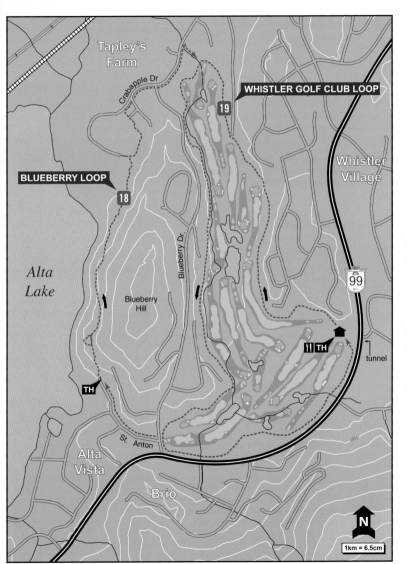

20 Village Exploration Walk . . . . . ☐

STATS: 2.7km, 49m, Year-round, N50 06.896 W122 57.374

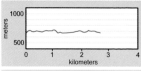

Three walking tours of Whistler Village have been included in this guidebook to help familiarize visitors with the area. The Village Exploration Walk is the longest and most diverse. Most of Whistler Village is designated "pedestrian-only" making it a great (and safe) place to stroll around, but there's much more to see than just the plethora of shops. The village is adjacent to parks, nature trails, waterways and golf courses, all of which add to the unique outdoor ambiance of the area. The Whistler Village plan was conceived by landscape architect Eldon Beck to preserve several mountain-view corridors and create pedestrian catchment areas where people naturally stop and gather. It's a great place to relax and the following walk provides a short "hiking" option that has very little elevation gain.

Access: *Start at Village Square. This pedestrian-only space was the original nerve centre of the village and remains a favorite meeting place. It is adjacent to a liquor store, grocery store, pharmacy and the iconic Whistler restaurant, Araxi.*

Map: *Page 90*

Walking: Start in Village Square.

▭▷ From Village Square, walk along Village Stroll, toward the base of Whistler Mountain. You will pass multiple stores and cafes before entering Mountain Square. The Carleton Lodge is the main landmark at the head of Mountain Square. Walk to the left of Carleton Lodge and enter Skier's Plaza at the base of the Blackcomb Excalibur Gondola, Fitzsimmons Express and Whistler Village Gondola. **Tip:** When at Skier's Plaza in the summer, pause for a moment to watch the mountain bikers as they finish their rapid descents of Whistler Mountain. It may inspire you to rent a bike tomorrow!

▭▷ From Skier's Plaza, locate the Pan Pacific Hotel and walk up the stairs between it and the gondola.

▭▷ From the top of the stairs, turn left onto the in-

▶▶

terlocking brick sidewalk and follow it to the crosswalk at Blackcomb Way.

▷ Cross Blackcomb Way and locate the broad, paved Fitzsimmons Trail between the parking lots.

▷ After a short distance, turn left onto Dry Creek Trail and follow it past the Dirt Jump and Skateboard Parks to the Valley Trail by Lorimer Road.

▷ Turn right onto the Valley Trail and follow it across the bridge towards Blackcomb Way.

▷ Cross Blackcomb Way and, once on the sidewalk, turn right and walk a short distance to the drive leading to the majestic Fairmont Chateau Whistler.

▷ Walk up the drive toward the Chateau and turn right onto the interlocking brick walkway between the Chateau and the Glacier Lodge. ▸▸

Interesting fact: Village Square has been the site of many historic events such as the welcome home ceremony for local gold medalist Ross Rebagliati in 1998, a near-riot on New Year's Eve in 2002 and the live announcement that Whistler won the bid to host several events for the 2010 Olympics.

Village Exploration Walk *From left: Strolling through the village on a clear fall day; outdoor art at the Peace Park.*

▭▷ Follow this walkway to the Wizard Express chairlift on Blackcomb Mountain.

▭▷ From the base of the Wizard, walk past Merlin's pub to the top of the staircase leading below the Blackcomb Way underpass.

▭▷ Walk down the stairs, through the tunnel and follow Fitzsimmons Trail across the covered footbridge over Fitzsimmons Creek. Once over the bridge, the popular picnic spot Rebagliati Park will be on your right and Peace Park will be on your left. Take the time to investigate both of these lovely spots. Peace Park is complete with lounge chairs and public art and Rebagliati Park is set within a beautiful stand of old growth forest.

▭▷ Continue walking along Fitzsimmons Trail, crossing a little footbridge to the crosswalk at the T-intersection of Blackcomb Way and Sundial Crescent.

▭▷ Cross Blackcomb Way and then cross Sundial Crescent. Walk about 3 meters along the sidewalk on Blackcomb Way and locate the secret stairs on your left leading down beside the Whistler Village Inn and Suites.

▭▷ Head down the steps and walk into an open court, known as Village Common, beside one of the many Starbucks in the municipality.

▭▷ Walk through the court and descend three short flights of stairs before turning left onto Village Stroll.

▭▷ Village Stroll will lead you past rows of storefronts, back to Village Square.

Interesting fact: Local snowboarder Ross Rebagliati made headlines on February 8, 1998 when he won the gold medal in giant slalom at the Nagano Olympics. Two days later, Rebagliati was stripped of the gold after testing positive for marijuana. Shocked and claiming that he had not smoked marijuana since 1997, he appealed the ruling. Rebagliati theorized that he must have inhaled secondhand smoke while at a Whistler party that January.

Medical experts agreed that the story was plausible given the low amount of marijuana that appeared in his system. The following day, The Olympic Court for Arbitration of Sport ruled that they did not "specify that marijuana is a forbidden substance" and therefore had no authority to strip the medal. With gold in hand, Ross returned to Whistler, the source of the secondhand smoke, as a hero. Soon after, the *Rebagliati Park* was named in his honor.

Whistler Village *Fall colours (top); returning from a rafting adventure.*

21 Village Centre Walk . . . . ☐

STATS: 2.2km, 54m, Year-round, N50 06.896 W122 57.374

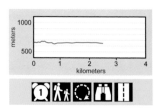

This walk is a great orientation to the entire Whistler Village.

Walking: Start in Village Square. Stand looking toward the ski areas and walk left along Village Stroll.

Access: *Start at Village Square as for the Village Exploration Walk.*

Map: *Page 90*

⟹ Meander along Village Stroll as it bends left and enters the open area marked as Village Common.

⟹ Follow Village Stroll onto the footbridge above Village Gate Boulevard. **Tip**: The footbridge is one of the most popular photo opportunities in the Village. There are nice views of Blackcomb to the east and Sproatt and Rainbow Mountains to the west.

⟹ Continue across the footbridge and walk along Village Stroll through the Town Plaza (complete with gazebo and granite boulders) to another footbridge, lined with public art, over a man-made waterway.

⟹ Cross the footbridge and continue along Village Stroll past the Whistler Celebration Plaza until you see a children's play area ahead on your right. **Tip**: This section of the village is a favorite for children. The interactive art on the footbridge over the waterway is always a hit and there is a really cool wooden structure complete with slide at the play area!

⟹ Just before you reach the play area, take the diagonal trail to the right between the Celebration Plaza and the backside of a row of shops.

⟹ Follow the trail between the row of shops (the post office will be on your right) to the outdoor mall called Marketplace.

▸▸

☞ Once between the buildings, turn left and walk along the sidewalk in front of the stores. Continue along the sidewalk until you can turn left between KFC and a café onto Main Street.

☞ Turn right, and walk along the sidewalk on Main Street to the intersection with Northlands Boulevard.

☞ Cross Main Street and walk along Northlands Boulevard to the intersection with Village Gate Boulevard. Enjoy the exceptional views of Whistler and Blackcomb Mountains from this intersection!

☞ Cross Northlands Boulevard and then cross Village Gate Blvd. Walk straight ahead on the sidewalk beside Whistler Way and follow it as it bends to the right.

☞ Stroll along the sidewalk on Whistler Way, avoiding the tunnel under the highway to the Whistler Golf Club, until you get to the driving range.

☞ As soon as you have passed the driving range, cross Whistler Way at the crosswalk before reaching the Westin Resort and Spa and walk up the sidewalk beside the interlocking brick-laden Springs Lane to the base of the Whistler Village Gondola.

☞ From here, you can walk back to Village Square or return to any part of the Village you want to investigate further. After all, you're an expert now!

Village Images *Clockwise from left: Unique water fountain; lunch in one of the village's many outdoor bistros; view down the waterway; beautifying the necessities.*

22 Village Park Walk . . . . ☐

STATS: 2.2km, 61m, Year-round, N50 06.896 W122 57.374

Village Park Walk is a meandering, interpretive walkway that cuts through the middle of the Village. It features several pieces of public art, a storytelling chair and a reading circle. This is a great walk for kids!

Walking: Start in Village Square looking toward the ski areas. Walk to your left along Village Stroll.

⇨ Meander along Village Stroll as it bends left and enters the open area marked as Village Common.

⇨ Follow Village Stroll onto the footbridge above Village Gate Blvd. **Tip**: The footbridge over Village Gate Boulevard is one of the most popular photo opportunities in the Village. There are nice views of Blackcomb to the east and Sproatt and Rainbow Mountains to the west.

⇨ Continue across the footbridge and walk along Village Stroll through the Town Plaza (complete with gazebo and granite boulders) to another footbridge.

⇨ Before crossing the footbridge, turn right and walk beside the watercourse lined with grassy lawns until you reach the copper-roofed Maurice Young Millennium Place. Known as MY Place, this is Whistler's centre for the arts and community gatherings.

⇨ From MY Place, walk around to the end of the watercourse, beside the vertically aligned basalt columns. Look at the paving stones complete with glass snowflakes within the columns. It is a display created by Celine Rich in 1998 titled Glacial Traces.

⇨ Walk along the watercourse back to the footbridge. Take the time to enjoy the interactive art that ▶▶

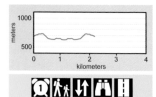

Access: Start at Village Square as for the Village Exploration Walk.

Map: Page 90

Village Park Walk *Clockwise from below: Storyteller's Chair; glass snowflakes; basalt columns make great climbing structures; summer banners.*

is installed on the railings of the bridge. These pieces of art comprise an exhibit entitled Sightlines (Kip Jones, Jennifer Macklem, 1998).

▷ Step off the bridge and continue walking along the watercourse to Main Street.

▷ Cross Main Street and locate the interlocking brick walkway leading into the forested Village Park Central. There is an interpretative sign and map located at the trailhead. This part of the park is known as the Karuizawa Friendship Walk and is dedicated to Whistler's sister city in Japan.

▷ Walk along the interlocking brick pathway and look for the large stumps with notches cut in them. These notches were part of a pioneer logging practice. A springboard was placed in the notch to allow the cutter higher access to the trunk. You will also be able to see the Reading Circle and Birdhouse Project in the trees on your left. The birdhouses were created in a family workshop under the watchful eye of local artist Isobel MacLaurin. Eventually you will arrive at the metallic Whistler Wayfinder exhibit dangling over a pond. It was created by Dwight Atkinson in 2000.

▷ From the Whistler Wayfinder, walk across Northlands Boulevard and stroll past two ponds into Village Park West. Walk up to the top of the Spiral Mound to the Storyteller's Chair (Carlos Basanta). The chair has the phrase "Once upon a time" in 30 languages embedded into the structure.

▷ As you walk back down from the mound, look for the marble Drinking Fountain (Simone Weber Luckham, 2000) near Northlands Boulevard on your left. After all, how often do you get to drink from a work of art! Retrace your route back to the start.

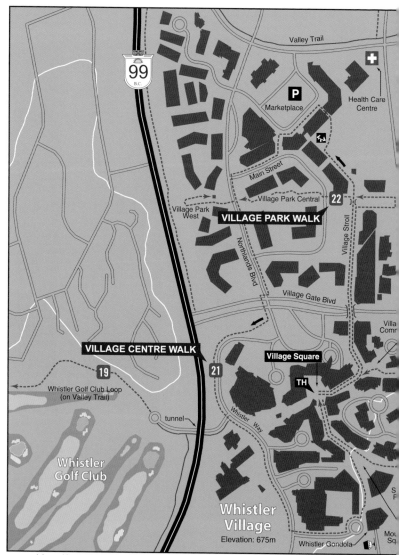

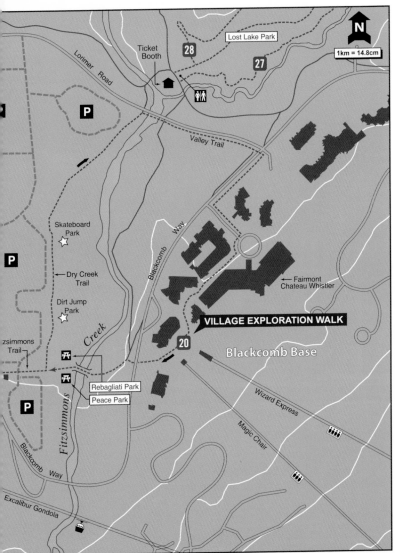

N

1km = 14.8cm

Lost Lake Park

Lorimer Road

Ticket Booth

28

27

P

Valley Trail

Skateboard Park

Blackcomb Way

P

Dry Creek Trail

Dirt Jump Park

Fairmont Chateau Whistler

VILLAGE EXPLORATION WALK

zsimmons Trail

Creek

20

Blackcomb Base

Rebagliati Park

Peace Park

Fitzsimmons

P

Wizard Express

Blackcomb Way

Magic Chair

Excalibur Gondola

WHERE WILL IT TAKE YOU?

THE OPTIONS ARE ENDLESS. With easy access to over 20 trails ranging from effortless to epic, the only challenge you'll experience here is the one you came for. The world record-breaking, new PEAK 2 PEAK Gondola transports you high above the valley between Whistler and Blackcomb Mountains' expansive alpine terrain, getting you closer to getting away from it all.

1.800.766.0449
whistlerblackcomb.com/summer

23 Singing Pass & Russet Lake Via the Musical Bumps ★★★ . . . . ☐

STATS: 27.8km, 1441m, July–October, N50 06.790 W122 57.141

This is a classic hike through wildflower-filled meadows to an alpine lake. The trail takes you into Garibaldi Provincial Park and affords rewarding views of the jagged peaks and glaciers of the area. It is highly recommended and deservedly popular.

Hiking: From the top of the Peak Chair, locate the start of Matthew's Traverse and walk to the junction with Burnt Stew Trail. Turn right onto Burnt Stew. Follow the broad, rocky road under the northeast slope of Piccolo, the first of the three alpine sub-peaks known as the Musical Bumps, and look carefully for a singletrack leaving the road on your left. Follow the singletrack under the Symphony Express (just above tower 19) and walk to a junction of trails marked with a signpost. Get onto the Musical Bumps Trail and follow the arrow "To Signing Pass." The trail will lead you over Flute and Oboe before descending to the junction with the well-worn Singing Pass Trail. Turn right at the trail junction and walk a short distance to Singing Pass proper, which is marked with an interpretative sign describing the local wildflowers.

From here, the walk to Russet Lake is about another 45 minutes to an hour. If you are running late or low on energy, consider skipping the trip to the lake and heading straight down the Singing Pass Trail to Whistler Village. To continue to the lake, follow the trail as it switchbacks uphill. The stunning view of Russet Lake and the Himmelsbach Hut framed by the Spearhead Range will be your reward. Enjoy the setting before returning to Singing Pass and descending the trail to Whistler Village. Make sure you save some energy for the descent, it's a long way down! ▸▸

Access: *Start at the top of the Peak Chair on Whistler Mountain.*

To Get There: *Ride the Whistler Village Gondola to the Round-house on Whistler Mountain. From the Roundhouse, follow the well-marked Peak Chair Traverse to the bottom of the Peak Chair and get on the lift.*

Map: *Page 103*

Singing Pass *Clockwise from above: Red Columbine; Arctic Lupine line the trail in Singing Pass meadow; Himmelsbach Hut at Russet Lake.*

Singing Pass *Clockwise from above left: Forest hiking on Singing Pass Trail; Whistler Mountain gondola: approaching Russet Lake with the hut at the far end; Indian Paintbrush in alpine meadows.*

Chairlift Timing: Historically, the Whistler Village Gondola has opened at 10:00 am and the Peak Chair at 11:00 am. Unfortunately, these times do not allow hikers to get an early start on their day. You can, of course, walk up the Singing Pass Trail from Whistler Village to Russet Lake. (The trailhead is at the Fitzsimmons Bus Loop.) This variation will save you the cost of the gondola ticket but is in some ways less rewarding. It is a 29 kilometer return trip, and you will spend much less of your day in the alpine, where the true splendor of the park is on display. Besides, not only Europeans should have the pleasure of being whisked to the mountaintops and walking dramatic routes in the high alpine!

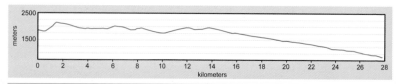

24 High Note Trail ★★★ . . . . ☐

STATS: 9.5km, 341m, July–October, N50 03.547 W122 57.469

High Note Trail is the highlight of the Whistler Black-comb hiking experience. Starting high on the south flank of Whistler Mountain the trail affords views of the iconic Black Tusk, the stunning peaks of Garibaldi Provincial Park and the emerald waters of Cheakamus Lake. This is by far the best walk on Whistler as it takes you away from the somewhat industrial feel of being at a ski hill.

Hiking: The trail starts at the top of the Peak Chair behind the stone Inukshuk at an elevation of 2,182 meters. It winds through the rocks before dropping elevation and contouring east on a bench at 1,900 meters across the small peak known as Piccolo. On this section of trail you will be rewarded with unobstructed views across to the massive glaciers and peaks towering ▶▶

Access: *Top of the Peak Chair, same as for Singing Pass Trail.*

Map: *Page 103*

Interesting Fact: The population of Hoary Marmots that live in the alpine can frequently be heard whistling at hikers that pass by on the trail. This trilling call warns the rest of the colony of potential danger and is the original namesake of Whistler Mountain.

over Cheakamus Lake. The trail eventually hooks back into the ski area proper at the col between Piccolo and Flute at which point the trail merges with the Musical Bumps Trail. Follow the Musical Bumps Trail downhill to the junction with the Harmony Meadows Trail which leads back to the Roundhouse.

Note: For hikers with limited time or energy there is a midway exit option called **Half Note Trail**. This alternative route splits off High Note Trail just before it disappears behind Piccolo and traverses above Sun Bowl. Half Note Trail returns hikers to Pikas Traverse below the Harmony Tea Hut and shaves a little over 2 kilometers off the length of the High Note Trail. It can be a handy escape if the weather takes a turn for the worse.

High Note Trail *Clockwise from left: High Note hikers admiring the view; the pale green waters of Cheakamus Lake in the valley far below; summer snow in the Whistler alpine.*

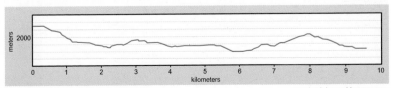

25 Harmony Lake Loop ★★ . . . . . ☐

STATS: 3.3km, 119m, July–October, N50 04.099 W122 56.625

This is an excellent objective for hikers wanting to sample the splendor of the Whistler alpine.

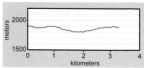

Hiking: Follow the broad trail beneath the snowmaking reservoir and begin the gradual descent to Harmony Lake. Once at the lake, continue downhill and walk the combination of singletrack and boardwalk around the main Harmony Lake and the smaller lakes below. From the south end of the lakes, continue up the talus slope to loop around the Harmony Meadows section of trail. The combination of the lake loop and meadows trail make for a nice short hike at the treeline elevation on Whistler Mountain with stellar views of Blackcomb's Lakeside Bowl across the valley.

Access: Start the hike at the top of the Emerald Express.

To Get There: Ride the Whistler Village Gondola to the top. Walk past the Peak 2 Peak and up the small hill to the trailhead at the top of the Emerald Express.

Map: Page 102

Harmony Lake *Extensive boardwalks make for great hiking.*

26 Zhiggy's Meadow ★★★ . . . ☐

STATS: 9 km, 230m, July–Oct, N50 05.628 W122 53.982

Zhiggy's Meadow is a pleasant jaunt through subalpine meadows, passing through the scenic Lakeside Bowl. (The slopes that tower above the bowl can produce massive class 4 avalanches during winter!) It is *the* classic hiking trail on Blackcomb and was built by local trail-building legend Boyd McTavish in the late 1990s.

Hiking: The trail is well-built and consists of classic singletrack and flat rock-hopping through a few boulder gardens. Follow the trail past Lakeside Bowl to a loop through the meadows below the peak of Blackcomb Mountain. After enjoying the great views across Fitzsimmons valley toward Whistler Mountain, walk back to the Rendezvous Lodge. From the lodge, we recommend riding the spectacular Peak 2 Peak Gondola across the valley to Whistler and downloading on the Village Gondola

Zhiggy's Meadow *A stunning alpine walk.*

Access: The trail starts just above the Alpine Services building on Blackcomb Mountain.

To Get There: Ride the Wizard Express and the Solar Coaster Express to the Rendezvous Lodge. The trail starts behind the Alpine Services building which is the large, metal structure that usually has several vehicles and snowcats parked outside.

Map: Page 102

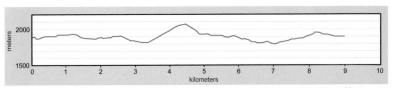

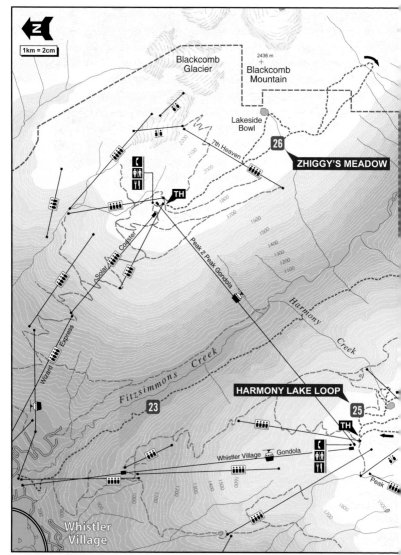

Blackcomb
Glacier

2436 m
+
Blackcomb
Mountain

Lakeside
Bowl

7th Heaven

26

ZHIGGY'S MEADOW

Coaster

Solar

Peak 2 Peak Gondola

TH

Wizard Express

Harmony Creek

Fitzsimmons Creek

23

HARMONY LAKE LOOP

25

TH

Whistler Village ⛟ Gondola

Peak

Whistler
Village

1km = 2cm

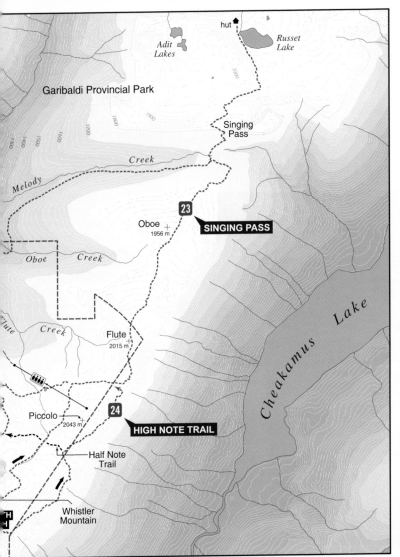

hut

Adit
Lakes

Russet
Lake

Garibaldi Provincial Park

Singing
Pass

Creek

Melody

23

SINGING PASS

Oboe +
1956 m

Oboe   Creek

Flute   Creek

Flute +
2015 m

Cheakamus   Lake

Piccolo +
2043 m

24

HIGH NOTE TRAIL

Half Note
Trail

Whistler
Mountain

27 Lost Lake Nature Trail ★★ . . . ☐

STATS: 4.1km, 69m, May–October, N50 07.197 W122 56.877

Lost Lake Park is a popular hiking and mountain biking area adjacent to Whistler Village. One of the best walking experiences in the park is the Nature Trail. It is a quiet, relaxing path on which mountain bike traffic is prohibited. The trail takes you past some beautiful sections of Blackcomb Creek, a couple of ancient cedars, and an intimate stretch of lakeshore. There are several benches along the way on which to take a break and enjoy the setting. ▸▸

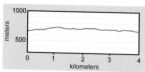

Access: *Start at the Ticket Booth.*

To Get To There: *From Village Square, walk along Village Stroll to Mountain Square. Walk to the left of the Carleton Lodge and enter Skier's Plaza. Locate the Pan Pacific Hotel and walk between it and the Sundial Boutique Hotel to Sundial Crescent. Turn right and follow Sundial Crescent to the crosswalk at Blackcomb Way. Cross the road and locate the broad Fitzsimmons Trail between the parking lots and follow it to the covered bridge over Fitzsimmons Creek. Cross the bridge, turn left (before going under the overpass) and then turn left again onto the Bridge Meadows Trail. This trail follows the creek to the bridge at Lorimer Road. Walk under the bridge, turn left at a T-intersection, and walk a short distance to the small log cabin (the "Ticket Booth") at the entrance to Lost Lake Park.*

If arriving by **car,** *park in the skier day lots by Lorimer Road and walk to Lost Lake from there.*

Map: *Page 109 and 91*

JIN YANAGIHARA

Hiking: From the small log cabin, known as the Ticket Booth, locate the trailhead for the Nature Trail near the outhouses. It is a marked with a post. The trail starts off next to Blackcomb Creek and leads to an intersection with the Lost Lake Loop. Immediately across Lost Lake Loop, the trail picks up again. From here, it continues through the forest, crosses another broad, rocky trail and eventually deposits you once again onto Lost Lake Loop just above the lake. Turn right onto the Loop and walk about 6 meters to the point where the Nature Trail starts again on your left. Follow the trail along the west side of the lake, joining Lost Lake Loop for a few meters to avoid a steep bank. At the north end of the lake, there is a memorial park bench, on a secluded point, that has a spectacular view of both Blackcomb and Whistler. Don't miss it! The Nature Trail ends here with a final junction with Lost Lake Loop. Turn right and follow the loop back to the Ticket Booth.

Lost Lake Park *Clockwise from lower left: Taking in the view from the memorial bench; casting for trout; a perfect dock for a summer dip; looking across the water from the Lost Lake Loop Trail.*

28 Tin Pants ★★ . . . . ☐

STATS: 4.3km, 90m, May–October, N50 07.218 W122 56.855

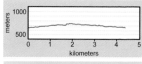

Tin Pants is a modern, machine built trail that winds through the forest at Lost Lake Park. The trail offers excellent sightlines through the trees and provides rewarding views of the village, Lost Lake and the surrounding peaks. It is a fantastic trail run option for those staying in the village! Note that one of the small trees along Tin Pants has been decorated with ornaments. Not surprisingly, it is known as the Christmas tree. It is always a highlight for children to "discover". We'll let you find it on your own!

Hiking: From the small log cabin, known as the Ticket Booth, walk about 20 meters along the Lost Lake Loop Trail and start looking for the Tin Pants trailhead on your left. It is designated with a signpost. The trail is easy to follow as it winds up gentle hills and brings you to the first of the benches along the way. Enjoy the view of the lake through the trees before continuing along the trail. Eventually you will arrive at a wooden gazebo at a small clearing. From the gazebo look for the Gypsy Drum trailhead. Follow Gypsy Drum to the intersection with Tin Pants and turn right, before descending back to Lost Lake Loop and the ticket booth.

Access: The trail starts at the Ticket Booth, same as for the Lost Lake Nature Trail.

Map: Page 109 and 91

Interesting fact: The trail's name comes from the canvas chaps worn by loggers and waterproofed with pine pitch. In cold weather, the pants often froze so stiff they were called 'tin pants'.

Lost Lake Park *Left to right: Yield to bears on Tin Pants; the twelfth "hole" on the Disc Golf Course.*

29 Whistler Disc Golf Course ★★★ ☐

STATS: 3.2km, 79m, May–October, N50 08.295 W122 56.827

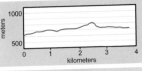

If you want to try a hike with an added challenge, Whistler has an elaborate disc golf course. Disc golf combines the fun of a walk in the woods with the skills of throwing a disc into a basket in as few throws as possible. The sport is rapidly growing, and the Whistler course is a rugged introduction for anyone keen to try their hand at something new. You can pick up a golf-specific disc at several local sport shops.

Hiking: From the trailhead, walk about 200 meters along the gravel trail to the warm-up tee. At the junction of the warm-up tee and the first tee, there is a map detailing the entire course.

Interesting Fact: *Disc golf has a professional circuit, and athletes carry specific discs for driving, sand traps, and even putting.*

Access: *The trail starts behind the Spruce Grove Park field house.*

To Get There: *Zero the odometer at the intersection of Highway 99 and Village Gate Boulevard. Drive north and at 1.8 km turn right onto Spruce Grove Way. At 2.1 km turn left onto Kirkpatrick Way. Park in the lots on the left.*

Map: *Page 108*

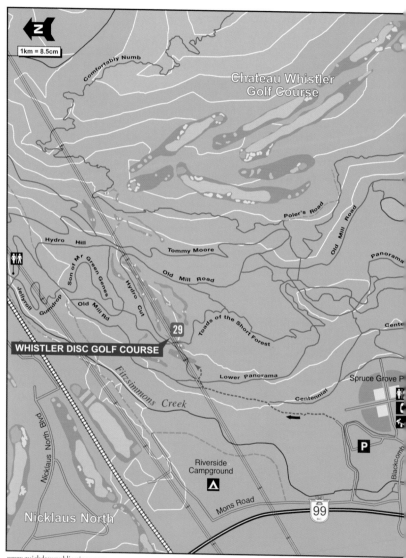

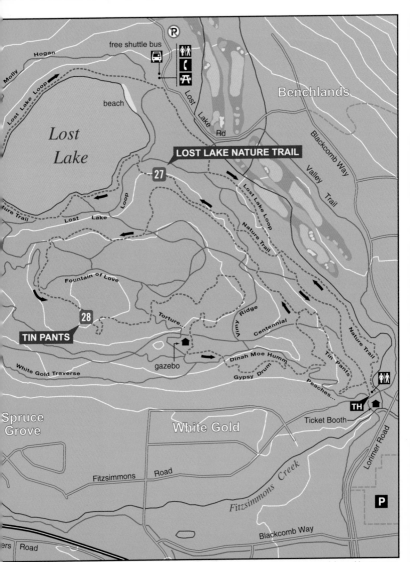

free shuttle bus

Hogan

Molly

Lost Lake Loop

beach

Lost Lake

Lost Lake Rd

Benchlands

Blackcomb Way

Valley Trail

LOST LAKE NATURE TRAIL

27

Lost Lake Loop

Lost Lake Loop

Nature Trail

Nature Trail

Fountain of Love

28

TIN PANTS

Torture...

Vinyl Ridge

Centennial

Tin Pants

gazebo

Dinah Moe Humm

Gypsy Drum

Peaches...

White Gold Traverse

TH

Ticket Booth

Lorimer Road

Spruce Grove

White Gold

Fitzsimmons Road

Fitzsimmons Creek

P

Blackcomb Way

...ers Road

30 Green Lake Loop & Parkhurst Ghost Town ★ . . . . . ☐

STATS: 10.6km, 254m, May–October, N50 08.518 W122 56.875

This is a nice trip with views of Green Lake and Rainbow Mountain. The highlight of the trip is a visit to Whistler's very own ghost town, the once thriving logging community of Parkhurst. Remnants of buildings, gardens, and vehicles exist from the 1950s, when they were last occupied.

Hiking: Get on the Valley Trail at the bend in Glen Abbey Lane and cross the train tracks toward the driving range. Follow the Valley Trail toward Lost Lake Park. At the entrance to the park you will see a posted map and a trailhead marked as "Hooktender." Follow Hooktender as it winds uphill, under both power lines, to a well-marked intersection with the "Green Lake Loop/Parkhurst" trail. Turn left (uphill) onto Green Lake Loop and follow the loose, rocky double track to an intersection with the Siwash Trail. Cross Siwash and continue walking uphill to a plateau above Green Lake. Eventually the trail will rejoin the power lines. Walk past the first hydro tower and continue along the trail until you reach the hydro tower marked "85-3" with a yellow plaque. This tower is atop a rocky hill. Descend the hill and immediately look for a trail leading to the left. This is the trail to Parkhurst. It is unmarked but apparent. Walk down to Parkhurst (check out the awesome blanket of moss that covers the ground on your way down) and follow the trail as it circumnavigates the ghost town. Retrace the route back to your car when you're done exploring.

Access: *Start your hike at the point where the Valley Trail meets Glen Abbey Lane near the clubhouse for the Nicholas North golf course.*

To Get There: *Zero the odometer at the intersection of Highway 99 and Village Gate Boulevard. Start off driving north on the highway. At 3.0 km turn right onto Nicholas North Blvd. Look for the Nicholas North Golf Course sign. At 3.6 km turn right onto Glen Abbey Lane (avoiding pulling into the driveway of the Nicholas North club house) and follow it around the bend to the parking lot. At 3.8 km park in the lot.*

Map: *Page 116*

Green Lake Loop *From top: Rafting in the Green River is a popular activity; abandoned cabin in Parkhurst.*

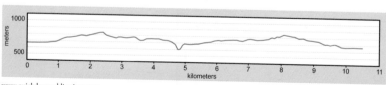

31 Comfortably Numb ★★ . . . . . ☐

STATS: 22.4km, 417m, June–October, N50 10.129 W122 52.950

Despite being designated a prestigious "Epic Ride" by the International Mountain Bicycling Association, Comfortably Numb remains a popular multiuse trail which has an annual trail running race. The route itself is extremely circuitous as it winds through the forest always following the path of least resistance. Note that Comfortably Numb is a *big undertaking*. There is no accessible water or consistent cell phone reception along the way. It is very important to be adequately prepared as the trail is *remote and rugged!*

Comfortably Numb finishes a long way from where it starts and requires forethought to arrange transportation needs. The first option is to leave one vehicle at the Lost Lake parking lot and drive a second vehicle to the trailhead. The second option is to lock mountain bikes to the concession stand rack at Lost Lake so you can ride the Valley Trail back to the trailhead parking lot after the hike. The final (and best) option is to get dropped off at the start and picked up at the end! ▸▸

Access: *Start walking from the dirt parking lot at the point where you turn off Highway 99 towards the Wedgemount trailhead.*

To Get There: *Zero the odometer at the intersection of Highway 99 and Village Gate Boulevard. Start off driving north on the highway. Keep your eyes open for the signs directing you to "(Garibaldi) Wedgemount" after passing the Emerald Estates subdivision. At 11.3 km turn right off the highway and, being cautious of oncoming trains, cross the railroad tracks and park in the dirt lot before crossing the bridge over the Green River.*

Map: *Page 117*

Hiking: Walk across the Green River bridge to the Wedge Creek Forest Service Road. Turn left, hike to a Y-intersection and then turn right, as directed by the sign to "Wedgemount Lake Trailhead." The partially hidden start of Comfortably Numb is only a short distance ahead on the right side of the road. Look carefully for a big green sign at the trailhead.

Follow the trail as it winds through the forest and crosses rickety bridges over marshes. After a gradual ascent, the winding trail will transition into a linear path that traverses above an old cut block and provides views of the Whistler heliport below. The trail will descend to an intersection with Young Lust (your last chance to get out), at which Comfortably Numb continues to the left. Cross the Wedge Creek canyon over the dramatic Al Grey Memorial Bridge. From the bridge, the trail continues meandering through unbelievable blankets of moss, eventually reaching a small hut designed to provide shelter while you have a bite and prepare for the second half of the journey. From here, the trail flows through the forest and at times offers dramatic views of Wedge, Blackcomb, and Whistler before descending to the Whistler Disc Golf Course north of Lost Lake. From here, well-spaced "Comfortably Numb" signs will keep you on route until you reach Poler's Road. Turn right, followed by a left onto Old Mill Road, which transitions into Lost Lake Loop. Follow it to the parking lot.

Note: Some of the bridges, boardwalks and rock slabs on this trail are extremely slippery, especially when wet. Use them cautiously!

Comfortably Numb *From left: Board-walks snake through the forest; a shelter provides mid-hike relief.*

Interesting Fact: The record time for running the route during the annual race is a scorching 1:49:50, achieved by Aaron Heidt in 2008!

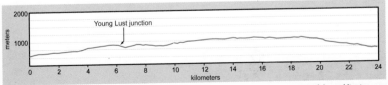

32 Comfortably–Young Loop ★

STATS: 8.5km, 273m, June–October, N50 10.142 W122 52.946

This loop is a combination of the first section of the epic Comfortably Numb and the Young Lust descent. It makes for a nice round-trip and allows you to get a sample of Comfortably Numb without having to endure its entire 24 kilometers! This is a *remote and rugged* hike. The trail incorporates wooden structures and steep, rock slabs that are extremely slippery when wet. It is appropriate for experienced parties only.

Access: *Same as Comfortably Numb.*

Map: *Page 117*

Hiking: Find the start of Comfortably Numb as per the *Hiking* section on the previous page. Follow Comfortably Numb as it winds through the forest and across some small wooden bridges. The trail will eventually straighten out and head southwest as it contours across the slope towards Wedge Creek. Just before you get to Wedge Creek, you will arrive at an intersection of trails. This is the junction of Comfortably Numb and Young Lust. It is well-marked. Descend Young Lust to it's conclusion at a rocky ramp that deposits you onto a dirt road. Turn left on the dirt road and walk down, under the power lines, to the Wedge Creek Forest Service Road. Turn right onto the Wedge Creek road and follow it back to the bridge across the Green River to your vehicle.

Added Value: If this is your first time to the junction of Comfortably Numb and Young Lust, make sure you take the short side trip to check out the bridge over Wedge Creek before you head down Young Lust. The Al Grey Memorial Bridge spans a really cool creek canyon and was slung into place by helicopter!

Young Lust From top: Crossing the Al Grey bridge, just beyond the Comfortably Numb–Young Lust junction; vivid green moss blankets the forest.

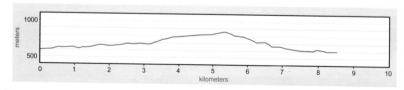

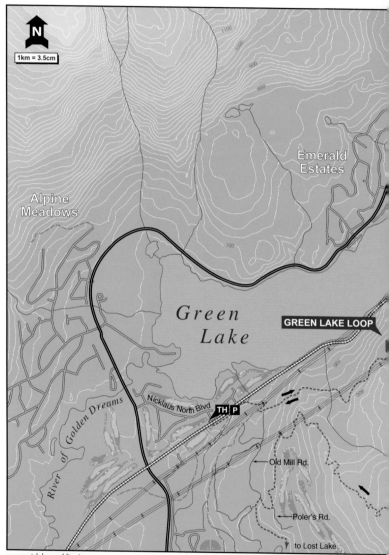

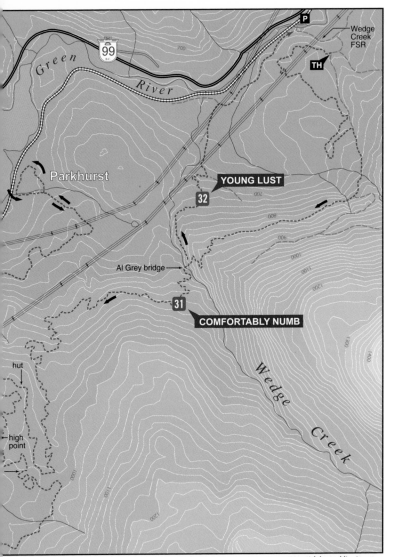

P

Wedge
Creek
FSR

99

TH

Green

River

Parkhurst

YOUNG LUST

32

Al Grey bridge →

31

COMFORTABLY NUMB

hut →

→ high
point

Wedge

Creek

33 Screaming Cat Lake ★★★ . . . . ☐

STATS: 18.5km, 823m, June–October, N50 08.658 W122 58.398

This hike takes you past jaw-dropping views of all of the prominent peaks in the corridor. It ends at a beautiful remote lake below the snowcapped Rainbow Mountain. Make sure you save this trip for a clear day as the views are the primary reason we place this trail in the three-star category!

Hiking: Start up the dirt road blocked by a yellow gate at the end of Alpine Way. Stay right at the first two intersections and continue uphill to the junction with the Flank Trail. Stay right at the junction. There is a small posting here with an arrow directing you to "Screaming Cat Lake 6.34 km." Follow the Flank Trail as it traverses the side of Rainbow Mountain to a crossing of Nineteen-mile Creek via a crude bridge. After crossing the creek, there will be a couple of opportunities to marvel at the view across the valley. Eventually, the trail will switchback steeply uphill and access the broad Sixteen-mile Ridge. After gaining the ridge, you will arrive at a junction of trails marked as the "Sixteen-mile Ridge Lookout Junction." From this junction, take the time to enjoy a short, side trip to a spectacular lookout from a dome-shape rock. It's only about a 10-minute diversion and well worth it. Return to the Lookout Junction and continue uphill for a little over 1 kilometer to a junction of trails marked as "Screaming Cat Lake Trail Junction". Leave the Flank Trail at this point and walk 1.3 kilometers to the lake. Return to Alpine Way by reversing the route.

Access: This trail starts on the dirt road blocked by a yellow gate at the end of Alpine Way.

To Get There: Zero the odometer at the intersection of Highway 99 and Village Gate Boulevard. Start off driving north on the highway. At 3.8 km turn left onto Alpine Way at the traffic lights. At 4.8 km Alpine Way ends in a cul-de-sac. Turn around in the cul-de-sac and find a legal parking spot on Alpine Way.

Map: Page 122

Screaming Cat Lake *From top: Autumn snowfall around the lake; Arctic Lupine blooming near the trail.*

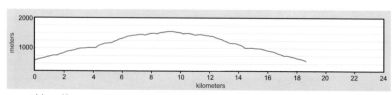

34 Ancient Cedars ★★★ . . . . ☐

STATS: 4.7km, 186m, June–October, N50 11.645 W122 57.573

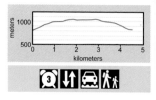

When we say ancient, we mean ancient! Some of the
cedar trees in this area are estimated to be over 1,000
years old and a few are over 3 meters in diameter and
60 meters in height. Sections of this valley were logged
in the late 1800s and, somehow, this stand of massive
cedars was spared. It is relatively rare for cedars to grow at such a high elevation (1,000m) and
these trees seem to stand here in defiance of the logging that occurred on the slopes below.

Hiking: Follow the rocky path up from the trailhead. After a short distance, a horse trail will
cross your route. Be careful not to turn onto the horse trail. Follow the main path until you
reach a T-junction with an old rocky road. Turn right onto the old road and follow it uphill.
The road will transition into a trail and lead to the cedar grove. The first large cedars that you
come upon are those that appear in the classic photographs of the area. They are a wonder to
behold and legend has it that you can gain strength by standing with your back against them!
Continue to follow the loop trail through the cedar grove until it brings you back to the main
access trail. Return to your vehicle via the access trail.

Interesting Fact: The Western red cedar was extremely useful to the native people of British
Columbia. They have been called the "trees of life," because it is from these cedars that the
aboriginal people obtained the materials for tools, shelter, medicine, clothing, ceremony
(totems), and transportation (dugout canoes). The native people were much more respectful
of the trees as a resource than the European settlers that followed. Rarely was a live cedar
cut down in favor of using the wood of fallen trees. At times, boards were harvested from
living trees by placing a series of antler wedges along the grain of pre-exposed wood. The
board was then pried off and the tree would seal the wound over time.

Access: The trailhead is just over 4 kilometers up the 16-Mile Creek Forest Service Road.

To Get There: Zero the odometer at the intersection of Highway 99 and Village Gate Boulevard.
Start off driving north on the highway. At 8.4 km turn left onto the unpaved 16-Mile Creek
Forest Service Road. At 8.9 km continue straight, passing the road to the Rainbow Sproatt Flank
Trail on your left and a tourism outfitter on your right. At 12.4 km pass a stable. At 12.7 km
park on the side of the road. The trailhead is at this point, marked with a sign and map.

Map: Page 123

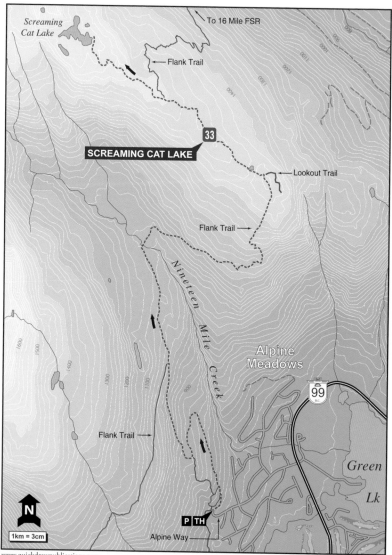

Screaming Cat Lake

To 16 Mile FSR

← Flank Trail

33

SCREAMING CAT LAKE

Lookout Trail →

Flank Trail →

Nineteen Mile Creek

Alpine Meadows

99

Flank Trail →

Green Lk

P TH

Alpine Way

N

1km = 3cm

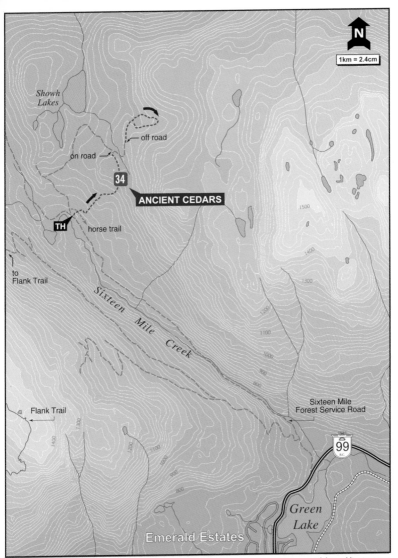

N

1km = 2.4cm

Showh
Lakes

off road

on road

34

ANCIENT CEDARS

TH

horse trail

to
Flank Trail

Sixteen Mile Creek

1500

1400

1300

1200

1100

1000

900

800

Sixteen Mile
Forest Service Road

99
B.C.

Flank Trail

1300

1200

1100

1000

900

800

Green
Lake

Emerald Estates

35 Wedgemount Lake ★★★ . . . . . ☐

STATS: 10.7km, 1154m, July–October, N50 10.302 W122 51.947

"Wedge" is the classic hike in the Whistler area and a right of passage for valley locals. It is a steep, rugged trail that leads onto a remarkable alpine plateau above the aquamarine waters of Wedgemount Lake. Views of Mt. Weart, Armchair Glacier, Wedgemount Glacier, and Wedge Mountain dominate the skyline and serve as a majestic reward to all who ascend to these heights.

Hiking: From the parking lot, follow the trail up a few switchbacks and cross Wedgemount Creek on footbridges. Now the real work begins. The trail climbs steadily through old-growth forest and past rock slides before eventually making a transition into the subalpine. The final section of the trail works it's way up beside a steep slope strewn with boulders and provides a final sting in the tail before leading to the shelter and campsite above the lake. When you get to the shelter, make sure you take time to enjoy the view! You've earned it after an elevation gain of almost 1200 meters. Return to your vehicle by retracing the route.

Access: Start the hike at the Wedgemount Lake parking lot.

To Get There: Zero the odometer at the intersection of Highway 99 and Village Gate Boulevard. Start off driving north on the highway. Keep your eyes open for the signs directing you to "(Garibaldi) Wedgemount" after passing the Emerald Estates subdivision. At 11.3 km turn right off the highway and, being cautious of oncoming trains, cross the railroad tracks and drive across the bridge over Green River. At 11.5 km turn left onto the Wedge Creek Forest Service Road. At 11.7 km turn right and head up a hill. At 13.2 km arrive at the parking lot.

Map: Page 126

Interesting Fact: *Wedge Mountain is the highest summit in Garibaldi Provincial Park.*

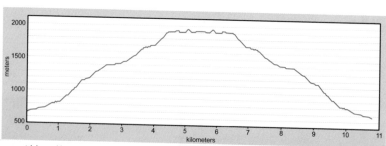

Wedgemount Lake *From top: View across the aquamarine waters; shelter with glacial ice behind.*

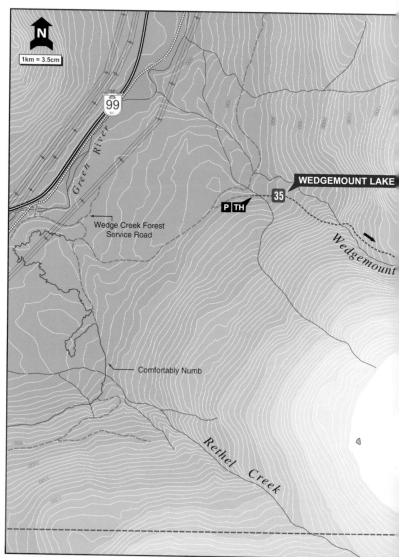

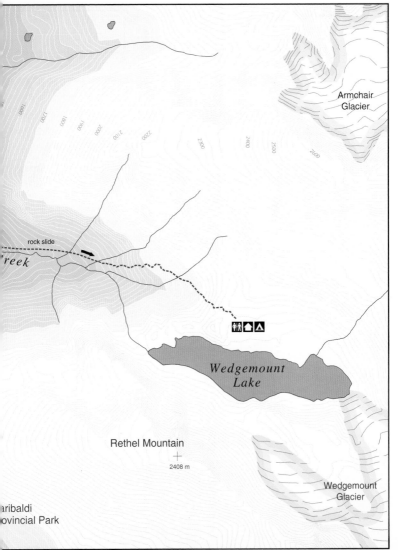

Armchair
Glacier

1600
1700
1800
1900
2000
2100
2200
2300
2400
2500
2600

rock slide

reek

👫🏠🔺

Wedgemount
Lake

Rethel Mountain
+
2408 m

Wedgemount
Glacier

aribaldi
ovincial Park

36 Nairn Falls ★★ . . . . ☐

STATS: 2.5km, 142m, May–October, N50 17.793 W122 49.228

This is a fantastic riverside trail that leads to an overlook beside Nairn Falls, a dramatic, double-step waterfall carved into the granite. It is a favorite for young families and older parties because it does not require the hiker to gain significant elevation. The viewing area at the falls has a bit of an industrial feel to it, complete with chain-link fences and warning signs, all in an attempt to keep people from falling into the turbulent water below. Regardless, it is a really cool place and a great walk.

Hiking - The trail is well-marked and leads upstream above Green River to the falls. Return via the same trail. ▸▸

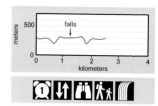

Access: Start at Nairn Falls Provincial Park parking lot.

To Get There: Zero the odometer at the intersection of Highway 99 and Village Gate Boulevard. Drive north and at 28.1 km turn right into the parking lot.

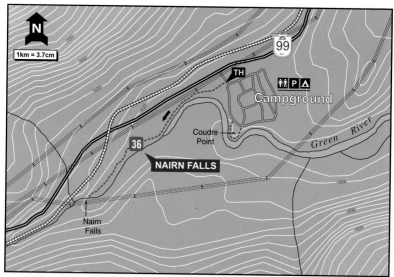

Added Value: After your visit to the falls, take the time to walk down to Coudre Point. This is a very short walk that leads down toward the river and gives you great views of the snowcapped peaks towering above. The point has a much more remote feel than the falls do. Locate the trailhead across the dirt road from campsite 17. The trail ends back on the road near campsite 47. Because of the proximity of this trail to the fast moving river, use caution and keep an eye on the young ones!

Interesting Fact: Believe it or not, the park is home to the smallest of the boa constrictor family, the rubber boa. This extremely cold-tolerant snake grows to an average length of only 45 centimeters. If you hate snakes, don't worry, the rubber boa is nocturnal and *rarely seen!*

Nairn Falls *From top: Water cascades over the falls; safe viewing area.*

37 Joffre Lakes ★★★ . . . . ☐

STATS: 8.9km, 361m, July–October, N50 22.162 W122 29.924

Pemberton is a small farming community nestled in a broad mountain valley about 30 km north of Whistler. In the summer, this area can get quite warm, but farther up the highway at cooler elevations is the Joffre Lakes, a mountainous region of considerable beauty. This hike is well worth the 1.25 hour drive from Whistler.

Joffre Lakes Trail provides access to all three of the Joffre Lakes and to an abundance of striking mountain scenery. The views from each of the lakes may ▸▸

Access: *Start at the Joffre Lakes Provincial Park parking lot.*

To Get There: *Zero the odometer at Highway 99 and Village Gate Boulevard. Drive north. At 31 km, turn right at the traffic lights. At 37.7 km turn right by the white church toward Lytton and Lillooet, staying on Highway 99. At 60.1 km, turn right into the Joffre Lakes parking lot.*

Map: *Page 133*

Joffre Lakes *From left: Idyllic camping at the upper lake; makeshift bridge; view of glaciers across the lower lake.*

Joffre Lakes *Waters in the Upper Joffre lake is tinged green from the silt-laden glacial runoff.*

be the most spectacular vistas of any described within this book. The hike into and alongside the lower lake is a great family objective (0.4 kilometers with no elevation gain) however, the remainder of the trail leading to the lakes above (4 kilometers with 400m elevation gain) is a matrix of exposed roots and jagged rocks *not* appropriate for families.

Hiking: From the parking lot, the first lake is only a short, 400-meter walk. The trail is mani-cured up to this point and continues a smooth course as it leads hikers above the south shores of the lake. Beyond this point, the trail changes personality dramatically as it heads uphill, over rocks, roots, and footbridges to Middle Joffre Lake. From here, it's more of the same! Cross back over the creek on the footbridges and climb steeply to Upper Joffre Lake. The trail leads to a rudimentary campsite at the north end of the lake where there are several flat boulders on which to enjoy a picnic. Return to your vehicle by retracing the route.

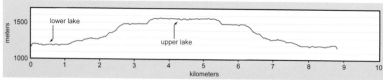

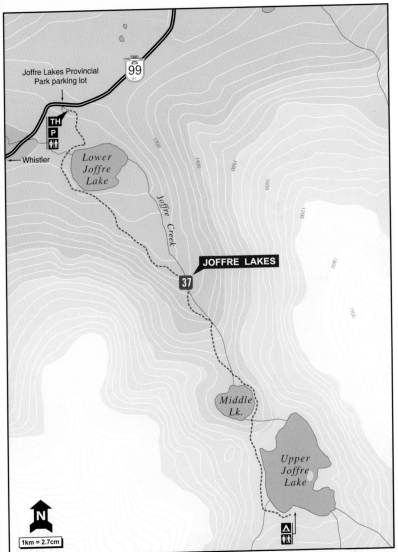

Joffre Lakes Provincial Park parking lot

99
B.C.

TH
P
🚹🚺

← Whistler

Lower Joffre Lake

Joffre Creek

1300

1400

1500

1600

1200

1800

1900

JOFFRE LAKES

37

Middle Lk.

Upper Joffre Lake

▲
🚹🚺

N

1km = 2.7cm

Rugged landscape *The volcanic remnant of Black Tusk dominates the skyline from Helm Creek Trail.*

CHAPTER 2:

WHISTLER GEOLOGY

Whistler is within the Coast Range of British Columbia, a spine of mountains that extends for almost 1,000 kilometers from North Vancouver to Alaska. The spectacular landscape of the region owes itself to a 150 million-year history of dynamic fire and ice.

This chapter outlines the four principal parts of Coast Range geology that are readily observable to those travelling on Highway 99 and hiking in the area.

WHISTLER GEOLOGY

The following text outlines the four principal parts of Coast Range geology that are observable to travellers in the Sea-to-Sky corridor.

1 **Granite forms the core of the Coast Range.** Granite is the gray, coarse-grained, crystalline rock (photo 1) in prominent outcrops along Highway 99 between North Vancouver and Pemberton. This rock crystallized from molten magma at considerable depth within the Earth's crust between 170 and 95 million years ago. It is now exposed at surface because of uplifting, and the erosion of the cover rocks.

The vertical rock faces of the **Stawamus Chief** (photo 2), **Shannon Falls** and the jagged outcrops of **Whistler Peak** are dramatic examples of this granite. The large pieces of broken rock that adorn Town Plaza in Whistler Village are fine examples of the local granite, if you wish to examine it in a more accessible form.

2 **Light gray to green volcanic rocks, approximately 110 million years old, flank the granite core of the Coast Range.** These volcanic rocks overlie granite in some places but more commonly, granite intrudes and includes patches of the volcanic rock (photo 3). Contacts between intruding granite and volcanic rocks are exposed at several places along Highway 99. These include the area just south of **Stawamus Chief**, the cutout for the Whistler Municipal Heliport at the north end of Green Lake, and **Nairn Falls** north of Whistler where there is a splendid display of washed and glacially polished outcrops.

The Resort Municipality of Whistler is almost entirely built upon these old volcanic rocks and the blanket of unconsolidated gravel and soil that locally covers them. Ski lifts on both Whistler and Blackcomb mountains traverse the volcanic rocks before crossing into granite near the top of Whistler Peak and Seventh Heaven.

These volcanic rocks have been badly broken by both faulting and intrusion of the granite. The flaky, yellowish rock on either side of the traffic light on Highway 99 at Blueberry Hill (photo 4) is an example of the former. Sheared and rusty outcrops at the Municipal Heliport exemplify the latter. The yellow-brown color (photo 5) is a result of rust, an iron oxide made during the weathering of the mineral pyrite. Pyrite consists of iron and sulphur, which upon weathering makes brown rust and, sulfuric acid that leaves yellow stains on the planar fault surfaces. The pyrite was deposited from hot waters circulated during faulting and probably contemporaneously with intrusion of granite.

3 **A second round of volcanism began about 100,000 years ago as the magnificent active and dormant volcanoes such as Mt. St. Helens and Mt. Baker in Washington State, and Mt. Garibaldi south of Whistler.** The most striking manifestation of early stages of this volcanic activity is **Black Tusk**. This dark spire rises high on the east side of Highway 99 and is first visible as one crosses the railway near the parking lot for **Brandywine Falls**. The best views of the Tusk are from the **Helm Creek Campsite** (Photo 6) and **Whistler Peak**. Black Tusk is a large erosional remnant of the edge and top of a dome-like edifice. Isotopic age determinations and evidence of glacial scouring place its eruption as pre-glacial.

At **Brandywine Falls**, and very notable in out-crops farther north where highway and railroad run parallel, the lava is broken into upright columns (photo 7). The columns, polygons in cross section, are caused by contraction as the lava cools and crystallizes. Such columns are much used for decorative purposes in Whistler Village and allow for close inspection. Look for them near the man-made creek between the Whistler Brew Pub and Millennium Place.

In the steps at the Legends hotel and the pedestrian bridge near the Creekside base, broken columns expose fresh black lava with baseball-sized bright green nodules (photo 8). These nodules are clusters of olivine crystals, a mineral that formed early as the lavas crystallized. Olivine crystals, where perfectly formed and unbroken are known as the semi-precious stone peridote.

Mount Garibaldi (photo 9) is our largest and most impressive example of pre-, mid- and post-glacial volcanism. The first good view of this volcano for the northbound traveller, in fine weather, is from a turnout 3 kilometers south of Shannon Falls. Stunning distant views can be had by looking south from Whistler Peak or north from the summit of the **Stawamus Chief**.

Mount Garibaldi began to grow more than 100 million years ago, before the last Ice Age, and last erupted 12,000 years ago with lava flows running down its flanks to chill and crystallize against glaciers. The west half of the volcanic cone is missing. It probably collapsed into the Squamish Valley when its underlying glacier melted.

4 **The recent history of today's landscape began about 20,000 years ago during the last Ice Age.** At this time, a vast sheet of ice and snow, more than 2 kilometers thick in major valleys, covered nearly all of British Columbia. By about 5,000 years ago the peripheral areas of this ice sheet melted. Evidence of this most recent glaciation is everywhere and at every scale. Howe Sound (photo 10) is a fjord, a deep, U-shaped, steep-sided valley carved by an advancing glacier and subsequently occupied by the sea as that glacier melted and receded up-valley. The round top and sloping east sides of the **Stawamus Chief** (photo 11) are the result of grinding, grooving and polishing by the great over-riding ice sheet. The Chief's vertical face is a truncation of outcrop by the glacier that filled the valley. The net effect is a half-dome shape, similar to that of Yosemite Valley in California. Grooved and polished surfaces on the granite around the Chief are exposed at its base and summit (photo 12) and are evidence of the passage of the glacier.

We can distinguish material dropped from the melting ice from that carried and deposited from running water of streams. The former is unsorted, not layered, and commonly consists of boulders in a matrix of sand and clay. These boulders are angular and have a flat side planed off when rocks are held in ice and dragged over underlying outcrops. In contrast, material deposited by running water is sorted as to size into distinct layers. Stream cobbles and boulders are rounded from banging together during their transport in running water.

The lakes of Whistler are a very recent part of the area's history of fire and ice. **Green Lake** (photo 13), so called because of its aquamarine color, most notable when viewed in sunshine from the heights of Whistler and Blackcomb Mountains, collects runoff from Overlord glacier via Fitzsimmons Creek. Such runoff carries in suspension fine angular rock particles ground by the glacier from fresh granite. Rock particles remain suspended for considerable time in Green Lake and reflect sunlight within the water. The net result is the aquamarine color typical of glacier-fed lakes. Green Lake drains northward via the Green River to Lillooet River, Harrison Lake, and the Fraser River to the ocean.

Alta Lake (photo 14) sits on the height of land between Whistler Creek and Whistler Village and drains to Green Lake via the River of Golden Dreams. **Nita** and **Alpha Lake** drain into the Cheakamus River and thence to Howe Sound at Squamish. Alta, Nita, and Alpha Lakes do not contain the striking green waters mentioned above because they only receive minor amounts of glacial water from Whistler Creek and tributaries that drain the Whistler Glacier, the shrinking patch of ice in Glacier Bowl. Whistler Glacier is within the older volcanic rocks and produces only a minor amount of powdered rock that settles in basins through which Whistler Creek steps down to the valley bottom. Solids carried by streams such as this are mostly organic material that absorbs rather than reflects sunlight. Hence the lakes are brown in color, not green.

Lost Lake (photo 15) is a special type of lake. It is not in the valley but rather on a terrace of unconsolidated glacial sand and gravel plowed up along the edge of a large glacier of which Overlord

Glacier is the retreated part. Lost Lake is rather circular, receives runoff from a radial display of streams, and has only a small and largely seasonal discharge at its south end. This is called a kettle lake. It marks the site of a block of ice that became mired, isolated, and covered in gravels at the edge of the retreating glacier. This block of ice ultimately melted and left a bowl-like hole into which local drainage has accumulated. It makes an ideal swimming hole (photo 16).

Drainage from glaciers through streams, lakes, and rivers continue to shape the landscape, always influenced by nature and structure of the bedrock. **Nairn Falls** (photo 17) on the Green River is one example. It is a series of cataracts, each several meters high and at right angles to one another. In the upstream part of the falls the Green River follows prominent near-vertical northwest- and northeast-trending planar cracks, or joints, in granite. On the downstream side of the falls the northwest trend is further emphasized by sheet-like intrusions of granite into older volcanic rock. This makes a complex yet linear contact between hard granite and relatively soft volcanic rock.

The Green River follows and erodes the rectilinear pattern of joints in the granite and the hard/soft contrast between granite and volcanic rock (photo 18). The net result is a zigzag-shaped waterfall well worth the short walk through forest from the parking lot.

Floral Splendor *A midsummer bloom in the meadows leading to Singing Pass.*

CHAPTER 3:

WHISTLER FLORA & FAUNA

At some point in our lives we've probably all been advised to "Stop and smell the flowers along the way." Well, the following pages are intended to provide further encouragement to do just that. The Whistler area is home to an impressive diversity of plant and animal life and the ability to identify some of them can greatly enrich your journey.

The following pages provide an overview of some of the most prominent flora and fauna in the area. So go ahead, take a second look at those tall, purple flowers before continuing through the meadow. Everyone will be so impressed when you call them by name ... Arctic Lupine!

-All photos by Jun Yanagisawa

FLORA

The identification of plants and wild-flowers in the region can be challenging. Several varieties of flowers look alike and one variety can sometimes vary in color and size due to exposure, elevation and blooming year. That being said, we have tried to organize this section as efficiently as possible. The following pages are arranged by the color of the flower. Since colors can vary, you may have to look within a different color category if you don't find the plant on your first try. Each

Winter no more *Summer flowers coat the Whistler ski runs.*

entry within this section lists the common name and the approximate flowering season of the plant. As you can imagine, the flowering season can vary greatly due to ground condition, weather, elevation, exposure and the amount of winter snow that remains.

Blue / Purple ❀

Arctic Lupine ☐
Proud and dramatic flowers found at all elevations through-out Whistler. (June to August)

American Brooklime ☐
Found in wet ground. (June & July)

Bird Vetch ☐
Generally found at lower eleva-tions with stems up to 2 m in length. (June & July)

Blue / Purple

Common Butterwort ☐
This flower is shaped to trap insects. It then secretes a juice to "digest" the tissue! (July & August)

Common Harebell ☐
A delicate plant often found in rocky, open areas. (July & August)

Douglas' Aster ☐
A beautiful plant with ray flowers originating from a yellow disk. (July & August)

Early Blue Violet ☐
Grows to 10 cm with heart-shaped, basal leaves. Found at low elevations to treeline. (May to July)

Pacific Bleeding Heart ☐
Delicate, heart-shaped flowers and basal leaves. (May & June)

Blue / Purple 🌸

Self-heal ☐
Named for its medicinal use by First Nations people. It is found at middle to low elevations in disturbed soil. (July & August)

Sky-pilot ☐
This plant grows from a taproot to a height of 30 cm at middle to high elevations. (July & August)

Slender Blue Penstemon ☐
Found in dry, often rocky or sandy soil at middle to high elevations. (July & August)

Thyme-leaved Speedwell ☐
A creeping member of the figwort family growing to 30 cm in height. (June & July)

Wild-flag ☐
A member of the iris family growing to 70 cm in height, with showy tri-petal flowers. (June & July)

Alaska Rein-orchid ☐
Look for the numerous flowers in a narrow cluster. (June & July)

Clasping Twistedstalk ☐
With oval-shaped berries of red, yellow or purple color. (June & July)

Brewer's Mitrewort ☐
Stems are from 15 – 40 cm with basal, heart-shaped leaves. (July & August)

Common Juniper ☐
An evergreen plant bearing small, blue fruit.

Green 🌸

Indian Hellebore ☐
EXTREMELY POISONOUS!
Ingesting a small amount will
induce loss of consciousness and
death. (July & August)

Pineapple Weed ☐
A pineapple scented herb found
in disturbed soil. (July & Au-
gust)

Stinging Nettle ☐
The hollow, stinging hairs of this
plant can cause an irritating
rash. (June & July)

Witch's Hair ☐
A hanging lichen often found in
old-growth forests. It was used
by First Nations to mimic hair
on masks.

Yellow Mountain-heather ☐
A low, matted herb with urn-shaped flowers. (July & August)

Alpine Willowherb ☐
Common at high elevations. (July & August)

Baldhip Rose ☐
Bearing red, pear-shaped hips. (June & July)

Bog Blueberry ☐
The berries may be covered in a waxy powder. (June to August)

Bull Thistle ☐
Primarily in clearings at low elevations. (July & August)

Red / Pink

Burdock
Common in disturbed areas, like roadsides, at low elevations. (July)

Canadian Thistle
Found at low elevations in fields and roadsides. (July & August)

Cattail
1-3 m tall stalk found in wetlands. (July & August)

Common Bearberry
Also known as Kinnikinnick, with bright red berries. (June & July)

Edible Thistle
A striking plant that can grow to 2 m. (July to September)

Red / Pink

Fireweed ☐
A striking plant found in disturbed areas like roadsides and avalanche paths. (July to September)

Fool's Huckleberry ☐
Drooping, bell-shaped flowers accompanied by deciduous leaves. (June & July)

Foxglove ☐
A striking plant with escalating, bell-shaped flowers. (June & July)

Fringecup ☐
A fragrant flower with toothed, heart-shaped leaves. (June & July)

Hardhack ☐
Tiny, rose-colored blossoms packed into a dense cluster. Found in damp ground. (July & August)

Hemp-nettle ☐
A weed with bristly hairs on the stem. (July & August)

Red / Pink

Indian Paintbrush □
The proud red flowers found at most elevations in the region. (June to August)

Marsh Cinquefoil □
An aquatic plant with reddish-purple flowers. (July & August)

Menzie's Pipsissew □
One to three flowers drooping off a single stem. (July & August)

Moss Campion □
Known as a "cushion plant" because of the dense compact mounds they form. Often found growing out of rock crevices in the alpine. (July & August)

Mountain Sorrel □
A member of the buckwheat family found at middle to high elevations. (June to August)

Nootka Rose
Flowers can bloom to 8 cm in width and can stand to 3 m tall. (June & July)

Oval-leaved Blueberry
A shrub with almost reddish branches and small, bell-shaped flowers. (May & June)

Red / Pink

Pink Corydalis ☐
A taprooted plant with flowers 10-15 mm long. (June)

Pink Monkey-flower ☐
An impressive flower growing in moist soil at middle to high elevations. (July & August)

Pink Mountain-heather ☐
A low, matted plant with bell-shaped flowers to 8 mm in length. (July & August)

Pink Wintergreen ☐
A striking plant growing to 40 cm. (June & July)

Prince's-pine ☐
Perfumed, nodding flowers on a stem growing to 35 cm. (July & August)

Red Columbine ☐
A member of the buttercup family with five, straight "spurs" pointing upward. (June & July)

Red / Pink

Red-flowering Currant
A flowering shrub with blue-black berries of 8 mm in length. (May & June)

Sickletop Lousewort
Look for the upper lip of the flower that tapers into an arched "beak". (June to August)

Rosy Twistedstalk
A perennial lily growing up to 30 cm in height, with bell-shaped flowers. (June & July)

Sheep Sorrel
A member of the buckwheat family, growing to 50 cm in height at low to middle elevations. (May & June)

Red / Pink

Salmonberry ☐

A flowering shrub that grows into a dense thicket and bears fruit that starts yellow and matures to a bright red color. (May to July)

Spreading Dogbane ☐

Identified by its milky sap and bell-shaped flowers to 8 mm in length. (July & August)

Swamp-laurel ☐

A small shrub with lance-shaped leaves to 4 cm and saucer-shaped flowers. (June to August)

Twinflower ☐

An evergreen shrub with nodding flowers found in low elevations up to timberline. (July & August)

Red / Pink

Western Coralroot ☐
An orchid growing to 50 cm in height at low to middle elevations. (June & July)

Western Dock ☐
A member of the buckwheat family growing up to 2 m tall in moist soil. (July & August)

Western Starflower ☐
A classy flower growing to 30 cm in height at low to middle elevations. (May & June)

Wild Ginger ☐
A low evergreen plant with heart-shaped leaves. (June)

Wood Betony ☐
An erect member of the figwort family with fern-like leaves. (July & August)

White ✿

Alpine Pussytoes
Identified by the several heads that grow in a tight cluster. (July & August)

Arctic Daisy
Marked by a yellow disk in the middle of the flower. (July & August)

Baneberry
A member of the buttercup family with shiny, red berries. (May & June)

Boreal Sandwort
Often found in rocky ground in the alpine. (July & August)

White

Black Alpine Sedge
Widespread in wet ground in the alpine. (June to August)

Buckbean
Found in wetlands and on lakeshores. (June & July)

Black Raspberry
A favorite of bears. (June & July)

White ✿ _____

Bunchberry
Flowers can also appear yellowish, purplish and greenish. (May to August) ☐

Candy Flower ☐
Growing from a taproot up to 40 cm in wet ground. (May to July)

Cotton-grass ☐
With a puffy "spikelet" at the top of the stem. (July & August)

Cow-parsnip ☐
Numerous small flowers in a cluster at the top of a 1-3 m tall stem. (July & August)

White

Crab Apple
A fragrant fruit tree adorned with white flowers. (May)

Devil's Club
A prickly plant common in the region. These guardians of the backcountry will keep you on the trail! (June & July)

Dogwood
A low, trailing plant with white flowers and red berries. (June & July)

White ✿ ──────────────────────────────

Douglas' Campion ☐
Usually found on dry slopes at lower elevations. (July & August)

Elderberry ☐
Bearing small, clustered flowers and red berries favored by birds. (May to July)

False Lily-of-the-valley ☐
Found in moist, shady conditions. (June & July)

False Solomon's-seal ☐
A broad leafed, delicate, white flowers with dull red berries. (May to July)

Field Chickweed ☐
White flowers that grow 8-12 mm in length. (June & July)

Foamflower ☐
Recognized by the jagged leaves with tiny white flowers growing from a thin stalk. (June to August)

Hooker's Fairybells ☐
White, bell-shaped flowers with tomato-colored berries. (May & June)

Fringed Grass-of-parnassus ☐
Five white petals originating from each solitary stem. (July & August)

Long-stalked Starwort ☐
A delicate plant with shiny, pointed leaves. (July & August)

White 🌼

Labrador Tea ☐
An indicator of moist soil, with evergreen leaves. (June)

Marsh-marigold ☐
*Found in moist to wet ground.
Flowers may have a tinge of blue.
(July & August)*

Lyre-leaved Rockcress ☐
*Often found in close proximity to open water or in moist ground.
(June to August)*

Northern Starflower ☐
*A pointed, star-shaped flower.
(June & July)*

White

Mooseberry ☐
A shrub with jagged leaves, small white flowers and red, single-seed berries. (June)

Pacific Dogwood ☐
A multi-branched tree growing to 20 m in height and bearing the floral emblem of British Columbia. (June & July)

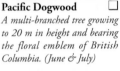

One-sided Wintergreen ☐
This evergreen plan has drooping, bell-shaped flowers and basal leaves. (May & June)

Rattlesnake-plantain ☐
Identified by unique, basal leaves that are dark green in color and mottled or striped in white. (July & August)

Round-leaved Sundew ☐
An insect eating plant with sticky, glandular leaves and small white flowers. (July & August)

White ✿

Salal ☐
A creeping shrub with dark berries and delicate, urn-shaped flowers. (July & August)

Siberian Bitter-cress ☐
A relatively uncommon species found on riverbanks at low to middle elevations. (July & August)

Saskatoon ☐
A shrub that can grow to 5 m in height. The fruit is red at first and becomes dark purple as it matures. (May & June)

❀ *White*

Sitka Mountain-ash
A 1-4 m tall shrub bearing small red fruit favored by birds. (June to August)

Sitka Romanzoffia ☐
Found in moist, rocky situations at low elevation. (July & August)

Spotted Saxifrage ☐
A matted plant with leathery, evergreen leaves generally found in the alpine. (July & August)

Spring-beauty ☐
Found in wet sites at middle elevations and recognized by its heart-shaped leaves. (June to August)

White 🌼

Star-flowered False Solomon's-seal
Bearing spherical, green / yellow berries that change to dark blue or black late in the season. (May & June)

Sweet-cicely
A member of the carrot family with sharply-toothed leaves. (May & June)

Sweet Coltsfoot
Growing to 50 cm in height in moist soil in the sub-alpine and alpine. (July & August)

White

Tufted Saxifrage

An often mat-forming plant growing from a taproot up to 15 cm at low elevations to the alpine. (July & August)

Tolmie's Saxifrage

A low, matted plant found near water in the alpine. (July & August)

Tea-berry

A dwarf shrub with bright red berries found in moist ground. (June & July)

White ❀

Utah Honeysuckle ☐
A leafy shrub bearing red fruit found in moist, open ground. (May)

Water-hemlock ☐
This member of the carrot family is so poisonous that a small portion can kill a cow if ingested! (July & August)

Western Anemone ☐
A hairy plant with large (4-7 mm in diameter) found in the subalpine to alpine. (July & August)

White Clover ☐
Found in disturbed soil at low to subalpine zones. (June to August)

White Rhododendron ☐
An erect shrub with "peeling" bark and flowers growing in clusters of 2-4. (July & August)

White Sweet-clover ☐
A fragrant plant growing to 2 m tall in disturbed soil. (July & August)

White-flowered Hawkweed ☐
An herb with milky juice and basal leaves growing to 120 cm. (June to August)

Woodland Strawberry ☐
An herb bearing small (1.5 cm across) strawberries found in wooded areas from the subalpine and below. (May to July)

Yarrow ☐
An aromatic member of the aster family with fern-like leaves. (July & August)

Yellow Willowherb ☐
A member of the evening primrose family with 4-petal flowers. (July & August)

Yellow / Orange ❋ _____

Big Deervetch ☐
In the pea family, found at lower elevations. (May & June)

Black Medic ☐
Adorned with small flowers in tight clusters. (July & August)

Butter-and-eggs ☐
An odorous figwort growing to 80 cm. (July & August)

Black Twinberry ☐
Look for the glossy black berries in pairs, or "twins". (May & June)

Yellow / Orange

Caltha-leaved Avens
A 5-petal flower found in moist soil. (July & August)

Canada Goldenrod
A perennial herb that can grow to 150 cm. (July & August)

Chocolate Lily
These bell-shaped flowers are marked with yellow or green spots. (May & June)

Glacier Lily
Golden, "recurved" flowers found in moist soil. (July)

Great Mullein
A biennial herb originating from a thick taproot, found at low elevations. (July & August)

Yellow / Orange

Hairy Cat's-ear
Distinguished by the secretion of a milky fluid. (July & August)

Heart-leaved Arnica
Found at low to middle elevations. (May & June)

Large-leaved Avens
A long-stalked plant with bright, yellow flowers. (May & June)

Mountain Buttercup
A compact plant found in the alpine and subalpine. (June to August)

Mountain Sagewort
A perennial herb usually found in the alpine. (July & August)

Yellow / Orange

Mountain Butterweed
A member of the aster family with ray flowers to 15 mm. (July & August)

Northern Goldenrod
An herb with spoon-shaped leaves and golden, ray flowers. (July & August)

Orange Agoseris
A member of the aster family. The "dandelion" of the mountains. (July & August)

Orange Hawkweed
Also known as Devil's Paintbrush and common along roadsides. (June)

Yellow / Orange 🌸

Pinesap ☐

This plant's name refers to the fact that it commonly grows in pine forests and secrets a sappy liquid. (June & July)

Pond-lily ☐

An aquatic plant with floating leaves and flowers. (July & August)

Prickly Sow-thistle ☐

A taprooted plant that secretes a milky fluid. (July & August)

Scotch Broom ☐

A deciduous shrub growing to 3 m in height at low elevations. (June)

Sibbaldia
A low, matted herb found at middle to alpine zones often in rocky soil. (July & August)

Skunk Cabbage
Named for its striking odor similar to that of a skunk, it is abundant in wet situations in the valley. (April & May)

Slender Hawkweed
A slender herb with basal leaves growing to 25 cm in the alpine. (July & August)

Spreading Stonecrop
A unique, mat-forming plant found in rocky soil at low to high elevations. (July & August)

Yellow / Orange

Trumpet Honeysuckle ☐
A climbing shrub bearing small, orange berries. (June & July)

Wall Lettuce ☐
A member of the aster family with milky juice, growing to 100 cm in height. (July & August)

Yellow Salsify ☐
A bright aster common at low elevations especially on roadsides. (June)

Western St. John's-wort ☐
Identified by the reddish, 6-9 mm long capsule-shaped fruit. (July & August)

Yellow Monkey-flower ☐
An attractive plant with large, trumpet-shaped flowers found in moist situations. (July & August)

Cheakamus Lake *Giant cedars and lush undergrowth frame the trail.*

FAUNA

If you come to Whistler in the summer months there is a good chance that you will get to view some of the resident wildlife. The black bear may be the "king of the mountain" but marmots, pikas and whiskey jacks also flourish in the area. One of the best ways to view wildlife is to take a trip up Whistler Mountain. On the gondola ride, you can often see bears grazing on the sweet grass of the ski runs below. This aerial perspective can provide an intimate, yet secure view of the animals and young hikers often find it the highlight of the day. Feel free to ask the lift staff at the bottom of the gondola if black bear sightings have been reported that day. The operator may be able to advise you as to what tower you should pay particular attention. Once in the alpine, a walk to Harmony Lake usually affords views of marmots foraging in meadows or sunning themselves on the rocks. Listen carefully for their telltale whistles as their coloring would make them hard to see if they didn't give themselves up with an audible signal.

The Whistler *A marmot sounds the alarm on Whistler Mountain*

Body Length: 120–210 cm
Shoulder Height: 75–90 cm
Weight: 90–270 kg

Black Bear
Although commonly black in color as the name would imply, these mammals exhibit a wide range of shades including light blonde and cinnamon. The Black Bear is classified as a carnivore although the majority of it's sustenance in Whistler comes from vegetation such as various fruits, berries, buds, leaves and roots. Females birth 1-5 cubs in January to early February. Amazingly, the cubs weigh only .25 kg at birth.

Fauna

Body Length: 100–190 cm
Shoulder Height: 90–105 cm
Weight: 50–215 kg

Mule Deer

These mammals are so named because of their prominent ears, like those of a mule. They feed on a wide variety of vegetation including seeds, shoots, berries, grasses, leaves and twigs. Mule deer can reach speeds of 55 km/h on land and are also good swimmers. 1-2 fawns per female are born in June or July with an average weight of 2.5 kg.

Body Length: 45–80 cm
Tail Length: 15–25 cm
Weight: 5–10 kg

Hoary Marmot

When sensing danger, the animal gives off a shrill "Eeeeeeee" sounding whistle. This piercing alarm is what provided the inspiration for the naming of Whistler Mountain. The word "hoary" refers to the grayish-silver fur on the upper back. The marmot is an herbivore feeding on grasses and green plants. It often eats snow to hydrate. Marmots mate shortly after hibernation and produce litters of to 2 to 4 young.

Fauna

Body Length: 70–105 cm
Wingspan: 180–230 cm
Weight: 3 –7 kg

Bald Eagle

Brackendale, 40 minutes south of Whistler, is the winter home to the largest gathering of Bald Eagles in North America, which is due to an abundance of migrating salmon. These birds of prey have bright yellow talons, beaks and irises that accentuate their white heads and tail feathers; juveniles are completely brown. Females lay 1-3 eggs per year and both parents take turns at incubation. The eggs hatch 35 days later.

Body Length: 40–50 cm
Wingspan: 50–64 cm
Weight: 450–750 g

Ruffed Grouse

Ruffed Grouse are omnivores that feed on buds, seeds, berries, insects and small reptiles. Their name is derived from the black "ruffs" on the side of their necks and colouring ranges from light grey to dark brown depending on habitat. This adaptability allows the bird to camouflage itself from predators. Females nest on the ground and typically lay 6-10 eggs, which take 3-4 weeks to incubate. The Ruffed Grouse doesn't migrate and has scaled toes, which extend to serve as snowshoes in the winter.

Fauna

Body Length: 18–20 cm
Tail Length: 2 cm
Weight: 75–290 g

Pika

Also known as "Rock Rabbits", these critters resemble hamsters with their stubby limbs and round ears. Pikas are herbivores and regionally survive on grasses, seeds, moss and lichen. They are seen in the alpine and at treeline carving out an existence on rocky slopes. Females have small litters of less than 5 after a month-long gestation period.

Body Length: 18–20 cm
Tail Length: 2 cm
Weight: 75–290 g

Whiskey Jack

These members of the jay family have learned that humans are an excellent "provider" of food and can sometimes be seen taking food out of the hand or off the end of a ski pole. Interestingly, this species lays eggs very early in the season, usually early March, when the snow is deep and the food supply is minimal. This is possible because of the large amounts of food that the Whiskey Jack stores throughout the summer.

INDEX

T

U

V

W

Index of Advertisers

This book would not have been possible without the support of the following quality businesses:

ACKNOWLEDGMENTS

Brian Finestone and **Kevin Hodder:** We would like to acknowledge the fact that several talented people have made valuable contributions to this book. First and foremost, we would like to recognize Marc Bourdon, our publisher, mapping guru, layout master and good friend. Without Marc's input and guidance we would likely still be talking about the idea for our first book instead of thanking him for his efforts on our fourth! Jun Yanagisawa contributed to this project in a significant way by allowing us access to his amazing archive of images and detailed descriptions of the local flora and fauna. Bob Hodder was kind enough to write the section on the geology of the Whistler area. Bob was involved in some of the first geological mapping surveys of the region and it's tough to find a better source of information! Ian Hodder helped with the technical editing of our text and was always willing to lend a hand at a moment's notice. Amazingly, he never even made fun of our basic command of the English language! Robert Kennedy routinely took the time from his busy schedule to answer our questions and support our project. You know, for a lawyer, he's a pretty cool guy!

The companies that chose to advertise within these pages have seen the value in investing in grassroots projects and we sincerely appreciate it.

A final thanks goes to our families, Abbie and Finn Finestone and Meredith Rozbitsky for tolerating the hours spent out on trail and in front of the computer. You have all made significant contributions to this book and we would like to simply say, "Thank you!"

Quickdraw Publications: A number of people made the task of publishing this guidebook much easier than I would have initially anticipated. The authors, Kevin Hodder and Brian Finestone, once again proved to be extremely professional in their approach and for that I am truly grateful. They provided excellent material and were very quick and efficient at responding to my plethora of questions throughout the process. Jun Yanagisawa provided a truly awesome collection of Whistler floral and scenic photographs for us to mine through. Like the authors, I feel as though his material added greatly to the quality of this book. Finally, my wife Pamela and daughter Elise were very accommodating in providing the necessary space to focus and put hand to mouse. Well, as accommodating as a 3-year-old could possibly be...

NOTES

ABOUT THE AUTHORS

Brian Finestone and **Kevin Hodder** originally met at college in the early 1990s. Kevin had worked on the ski patrol at Whistler Mountain and Brian on Blackcomb. They realized that their combined knowledge of the local geography would have value to visitors to Whistler and the idea for their first book was born. Their Ski and Snowboard Guide to Whistler Blackcomb – Advanced/Expert Edition was an instant success and has sold over 15,000 copies to become the best-selling book in the valley.

Brian and Kevin have climbed, skied, biked and hiked just about every inch of the Whistler valley while exploring existing routes and adding a few of their own. They both live in Whistler and contribute to the local community. They hope that the backcountry they have enjoyed for so long can remain pristine for generations of visitors to come.

Authors in Action *From top: Kevin Hodder on Mount Kenya; Brian Finestone surfing in Mexico.*